A BRIEF HISTORY OF WATERBURY

Edith Reynolds & John Murray

The History Press

Published by The History Press
Charleston, SC 29403
www.historypress.net

Cover image: The Carrie Welton Fountain, erected in honor of heiress Caroline Josephine Welton's favorite horse, Knight. From the authors' collection.

First published 2009

Manufactured in the United States

ISBN 978.1.59629.660.2

Library of Congress Cataloging-in-Publication Data

Reynolds, Edith.
A brief history of Waterbury / Edith Reynolds and John Murray.
p. cm.
Includes bibliographical references and index.
ISBN 978-1-59629-660-2 (alk. paper)
1. Waterbury (Conn.)--History. I. Murray, John, 1957- II. Title.
F104.W3R493 2009
974.6'8--dc22
2009008968

Notice: The information in this book is true and complete to the best of our knowledge. It is offered without guarantee on the part of the authors or The History Press. The authors and The History Press disclaim all liability in connection with the use of this book.

CONTENTS

PREFACE

Both John Murray and I are outsiders who opened businesses in town some sixteen years ago. We had an idea that we would contribute to this community. I use the term "outsider" in a Waterbury sense. Though I've lived here for thirty-seven years, I was not born in town. I'm not exactly a carpetbagger either, since both my daughters (Helen and Sarah King) were raised here and my husband, Dan Gaeta, is native-born.

I've heard this town called "the center of the universe" as well as "the armpit of Connecticut," but no matter how one might feel about the city on any given day, I know that those sobriquets are allowed to residents. Nonresidents who utter disparaging remarks had better beware. You see, Waterbury is a familial place.

Writing an overview of this city's history has provided me with the opportunity to look at the contradictory nature of the place. I find that there are no easy answers to simple questions and no singular way of interpreting what I saw.

For instance, Lisa Bessette (our café manager at John Bale Books) recently asked, "Where do you think things went wrong?" The answer seems easy enough since the most obvious cause is the point when the brass industry abandoned Waterbury. A more inclusive answer is: while the loss of industry was a watershed moment in town, the sense of helplessness really stems from a fear that we may not be able to recover, and that seems to derive from a sense that we do not believe we *deserve* to recover. And, that, in turn, causes us to devalue what we have.

For many years I've heard people lament that times used to be better. It's true. Good paychecks and job security have a way of making things good. We seem to forget that those plentiful times were also rife with pollution, people were periodically maimed on the job and a large segment of our population was ignored and treated shabbily.

I believe a look at the city today reveals a true promise.

Waterbury has an amazing array of architecture with charm and old-world craftsmanship. Yet we allow these structures to fall into disrepair.

The city hall is a prime example. When times were good, maintenance was pushed aside because there was always "time" to get around to things. When times got bad, city hall fell victim to the "rob Peter to pay Paul" syndrome. But fine things are not to be lightly discarded.

While the cost seems high today, accepting the responsibility for our heritage preserves something of value for tomorrow.

It isn't as easy to fix a city as it is to fix a building. Waterbury has serious problems. Other Connecticut cities and other American cities have the same problems. White flight to the suburbs and the exodus of industry eroded our tax base. At the same time, cities became a dumping ground for problems that outlying towns prefer to ignore.

Thank God for the generosity of spirit one can find in Waterbury. Churches, individuals and organizations work diligently to care for the homeless, the hungry, the tired and the poor. We also take care of the mentally ill, the sick, the paroled and the disenfranchised.

Volunteerism and community spirit keep Waterbury's heart beating, but too few bear that burden and those volunteers who toil often go unnoticed by the people who benefit from their time and talents.

Another thing I learned is that almost everyone in Waterbury thinks that he or she should be mayor. I don't know why. From what I can see, it is a task that's thankless, aggravating and discouraging. The skills needed to accomplish the job are multitudinous. Being a good mayor for Waterbury requires more than just a desire for the job. We have seen the damage wrought from poor choices. Pedigree and public access familiarity is not the way to select an able leader. Nor is following someone who is charismatic if he or she lacks practical skills. We as a city deserve more and should demand more.

As for ability, a modern mayor has to have fiscal expertise, the ability to manage people, diplomacy and a team of hardworking associates who provide an honest day's work.

I would never want the job. Even if I could learn the skills, I couldn't take the abuse. A while back, a woman told me that she was disappointed with Mayor Mike Bergin. Her disappointment had nothing to do with corruption, or his pay, or work hours or anything that really pertains to the good governance of a city. It was about squirrels.

Mike Bergin was not an expert in ridding a porch of squirrels.

I was amazed to learn that Mike Bergin actually took this woman's call. My amazement increased when she said that he told her to contact the UCONN Extension Service. Good advice.

Nope. The woman vowed that she would never vote for him again. Ever!

Why, when she had gotten through to her elected official and he had given her reasonable advice?

The woman was adamant. Mike Bergin was a terrible mayor. After all, she surmised, "A mayor should know about things like that. Those squirrels did a lot of damage."

It made me think that being a politician was the result of a DNA malfunction. Who would want that kind of telephone call when trying to balance a multi-hundred-million-dollar budget?

For me, I'll stick with my mother's advice: a city should be better because you lived there. That means, do something to the best of your ability.

I stick to volunteering, and I am pleased to report that I've met the nicest people. I am humbled by the qualities of leadership and genuine caring that so many of our citizens demonstrate. So many choose to turn off the TV and participate in neighborhood community clubs, work on bettering downtown, raise money for charity and launch new programs that provide a better experience for our children.

Our city is trying. The Mayor's Economic Task Force meets to recommend improvements; the Waterbury Development Corporation (WDC) oversees economic development and project management; the Citizens' Action Committee (CAC) recommends grants for social services; and the Connecticut Community Foundation provides financial assistance for myriad programs. There are many ways in which to serve the community, and I encourage anyone to make the attempt. Remember, it is *your* city.

If you are discouraged by what seems to be a lack of progress, remember that improvements take time. The wheel of fortune has gone round for Waterbury, taking it from a meager farmland to an industrial giant and then turning it back to a less substantial existence. Our job is to create the next stage on life's wheel and not wait for happenstance.

Of course, that doesn't mean sit around and wait. What is successful in our city today is what was successful in the past. The entrepreneurial spirit is the medium through which that next success will come. Someone, somewhere, is out there thinking of the next great invention. Meanwhile, there are countless entrepreneurs all around us working quietly. One of my favorite ventures blends a new idea on a historic foundation. Something very Waterburian.

The House on the Hill Bed and Breakfast seemed an unlikely venture in the 1980s, when times were first hard. Those in the Overlook and Hillside neighborhoods wondered what kind of people would come to stay in a city neighborhood instead of at a modern hotel. But Marianne Vandenburg had an idea that people might appreciate a stay in a historic Victorian mansion. She was right.

The house itself is a charm. It was built by the Camp family during the Victorian era and then abandoned when they built a larger home next door. Instead of razing the older house, they sold it to a family.

The house was large and had plenty of bedrooms to accommodate the new owners. Mayor Edward Bergin and his wife, Mary, had nine children and were known to take in relatives. The Camp house offered a lot of space.

After the children grew up and moved away, and after the mayor's untimely death, Mary Bergin sold the mansion to Marianne. The new owner set to work restoring the structure to its earliest details and configuring it as a refuge for weary travelers. Pretty soon other homes in Overlook followed suit.

More than twenty-five years later, the bed-and-breakfast is still thriving—a testimony to the fact that one cannot always predict success.

I end with my thanks to so many individuals whom I have come to know and respect. After that, I'll share a personal moment.

My sincere thanks and highest regards go to those who shared their great love of the city with me: John Murray, Steve Gambini, Gary Brodeur, Ron Guerrera, Ken and Brenda Killer, Phil Benevento, Mel Bergin, John Moriarty and Ellyn and Bill Scully. I thank those who work tirelessly for this city: Bonnie Orintas and Elaine Puzzo for their great contribution to beautifying the city; Rachael Guest for her informative blog, words and wisdom; all the volunteers from Main Street Waterbury; the WDC for its humble contributions, which include Leo Frank's leadership, Cathy MacNamara's great abilities, Geoff Green's steadfast diligence and Andrew Martelli's enthusiastic love for our city, as well as all the members of this organization who, sadly, do not get a fraction of the credit they deserve; Health Director Rose Wright for opening her archives; Peter Abare-Brown, who does double duty working for the city as well as serving as my ex officio marketing director; Senator Joan Hartley for her fine representation; the *Waterbury Republican-American* for reporting local news; the members of the CAC for working so hard to distribute federal block grant money fairly and thoughtfully to so many needy and deserving groups; the Connecticut Community Foundation for its tireless support of this community; the Arts Culture Collaborative and its many members who provide the uplift of spirit that any city needs; Shakesperience for providing Shakespeare in our park; the Mattatuck Museum for keeping our culture alive; those people who help provide our Halloween festival; the downtown merchants; Main Street Waterbury; the fire department; the police department; the fire marshal's office and the firefighters credit union; the Mayor's Council on Culture and Tourism; WATR; and our downtown ambassadors. And my heartfelt thanks go to Mayor Michael Jarjura for his time and patience. I especially thank my husband, Dan; my daughters, Helen and Sarah; the men in their lives (Shannon and Frank);

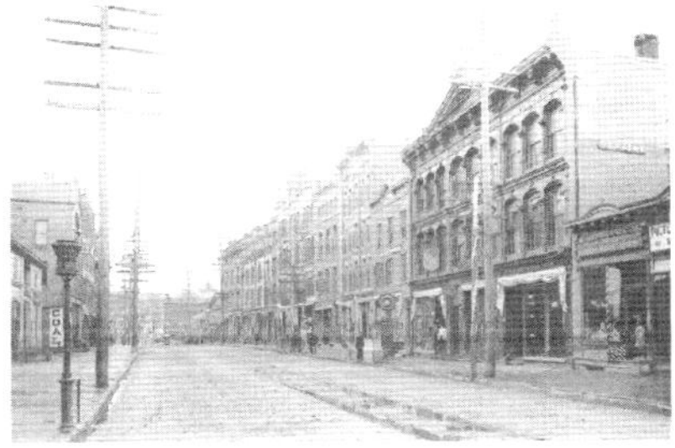

BANK STREET, NORTH
People prefer to remember the glory days when downtown was filled with shops and a buying public. *From* Waterbury and Her Industries.

my grandchildren, Thomas and Paige; and the John Bale Book Company staff who really made this book possible (Lisa, Krista, Lance, Vicky, Furlan and Terry). There are so many who deserve to be thanked and who have earned my gratitude and friendship. I ask for forgiveness from those I overlooked.

And now the personal moment. Very recently my daughter Helen signed up for Facebook, where she found a list of twenty-five ways you know you're from Waterbury. It's a tongue-in-cheek kind of thing that she read with her husband (who hails from Indiana farm country). She fully anticipated that there would be something embarrassing about the list, but instead she found that it filled her with pride.

She does remember Frankies hot dogs and hasn't found their equal anywhere. She does remember sneaking into the Fulton Park pool after hours with her friends. And, yes, she did hang out at the old mall.

It made her think about home, where she had a wonderful high school job at the downtown library, and of her boss, Mike DeLeo, who taught her that Waterbury was a city that created giants.

She recalled that while she and her husband were at Edwards Air Force Base in California, the shuttle was supposed to land with a Waterbury native aboard. Not many cities can boast even a portion of what Waterbury has—Hollywood stars, inventors, industrial leaders, writers, jurists, politicians and even a potential saint.

And at the end of the list she came across the one item that was supposed to be sarcastic—the man waving the flag in front of the mall.

Ziggy.

Waterbury's own.

Perfect.

Helen knew Ziggy. He befriended her son while he was in Waterbury. Ziggy bought Thomas a jacket, took him to patriotic memorials and marched with him in the parade. If anyone was going to be a symbol of the town, Ziggy was a good choice. After all, Ziggy's qualities mirrored those of his city: immigrant roots that blossomed into fervent patriotism, enthusiasm and kindness.

Chapter One

EARLY SETTLEMENT AND AN EMERGING NATION

Little is known about Waterbury (or Matetacoke, as the Native Americans called it) prior to the visit in 1657 of two white explorers, William Lewis and Samuel Steele. The land had been deemed unusable for habitation by the Tunxis tribe because of its propensity for flooding, but it was a useful hunting area with gently rolling hills formed by glaciers and a deep valley where the Naugatuck River wound its way down from the Berkshire foothills to Long Island Sound.

The first settlers moving into the area were a part of the overcrowded Farmington Plantation, and though the land proved barren of the mineral riches Lewis and Steele had sought, it had an appeal for farming. And so the allure of mining was replaced by the allure of settlement. *Matetacoke* meant "a land without trees" in the Algonquin tongue, but some could be found on the nearby hillsides for use in building cabins and providing staples like chestnuts. There were laurel bushes so thick that their branches could be used for making furniture. The alluvial plain around the river formed a natural prairie for agriculture. Water was plentiful.

As the name implies, water is the leading feature of the area. Aside from the Naugatuck River, the Mad River cuts through the eastern side of the city, along with two mighty brooks.

Early scouting forays reported the area as suitable for thirty families, and so a first settlement was started on the hilltops of the western shore, in what is now called Town Plot. The land was a flat hill plain overlooking the valley, a feature that the early settlers deemed advantageous for keeping watch for hostile intruders. Though an early deed was obtained from the Tunxis tribe, the lack of land ownership among Native Americans proved problematic for the settlers. After payment (thirty-eight dollars) was made, the settlers believed that the land was theirs for perpetuity, though repeated returns for money demonstrated that the tribe saw payments as little more than rental fees for the use of the hunting ground.

Hostilities grew as the European population swelled and placed continued stress on the land by expanding farms and hunting game. Native tribes like the Quinnipiacs and Paugussetts were continually pushed westward and northward from the shoreline, encroaching on territory staked out by other indigenous tribes unwilling to share. Tribes were decimated by disease brought from another hemisphere, and members fell victim to measles, smallpox and spotted fever until finally an eruption occurred in the form of King Philip's War, launched in 1675 by Metacomet, or King Philip as he was known to the Massachusetts settlements.

Metacomet did not share the trust of the new settlers that his father, Massasoit, and his brother, Wamsutta, encouraged, and he began plotting with other tribes against the Europeans almost immediately after ascending to chief. His family's tolerance of European ways was distasteful to Metacomet, who bristled at the settlers' religious restrictions against consorting with Native Americans. After Metacomet's European advisor, John Sassamon, betrayed a confidence by warning settlers that the new chief was conspiring with other tribes against the newcomers, Sassamon was found murdered, lying beneath the ice of a frozen pond. Three from Metacomet's tribe were tried and hanged, violating what the chief determined to be a breach of Indian sovereignty, and this provided the wily chief with an excuse to retaliate.

For two years a terrible war raged and spread beyond Massachusetts. The conflict wiped out large portions of the native tribes and frightened settlers into retreating to larger communities for defense. Waterbury was no exception, and the earliest pilgrims hurried back to Farmington, abandoning the Town Plot encampment.

At the war's end, in 1677, settlers returned to the Mattatuck area to restore the settlement, but rather than rebuild on the western hillside, the second wave of inhabitants chose to build on the eastern bank, where travel to and from Farmington would be easier. The choice was not the best, for arable land was far better in what are now Watertown and Naugatuck. Waterbury, as it came to be called, was marshy and pest-ridden. The threat of flood was ever present.

Waterbury's most densely populated area centered on what is now the town green, an area that, as everyone who has lived in town during torrential rainstorms knows, is prone to flooding. At the time, this parcel of land was little more than a bog. Settlers in the seventeenth century couldn't have chosen a moister environment, with the Naugatuck River floodplain less than a mile away, a smaller river and two brooks (the Great and Lesser). They were, it seems, the original "Swamp Yankees," so it is no wonder that an epidemic called the Great Sickness spread through the colony in 1712.

The town grew from rudimentary and humble beginnings. Cabins were built, and tree stump fences made it possible for individual homes to have stockades for defense, but the structures had little "curb appeal." A communal pasture for animals and one for farming ensured a food supply. As the community grew and became more established, water proved invaluable for starting a sawmill and gristmill, thereby diminishing the dependence on the Farmington community. In 1681, the town consisted of twenty-eight dwellings (fifteen of which were deemed "permanent" homes), twenty-two families with a total of ninety-three children, one household without children and six unmarried men.

The encroachment of Europeans continued to annoy what few Native Americans were left, and tribes took advantage of the political wars being waged between the English and French. Connecticut was first settled by the Dutch, who had chosen Hartford as an outpost from their stronghold of New Amsterdam. By the time Waterbury was established, the English, who moved westward from the Boston colony, had replaced the Dutch. As the English established a foothold in New England, the French living to the north offered the native inhabitants self-serving assistance in their plight and used the hostility to make mischief in the newly formed English communities. Mohawks living to the west were not the natives settlers feared.

In 1710, during Queen Anne's War, the settlers' fears were realized. First, Joseph Scott was ambushed and killed while tilling his land near Reynolds Bridge. Later, in a separate attack, Jonathan Scott (no relation to Joseph) and his two sons were surprised at Hancock Meadow by a group of Indians who attacked without warning. The two boys ran for help while their father struggled. Scott was overpowered and quickly subdued. His assailants promised to spare the boys' lives if they returned.

The boys did return to save their father, and the three were taken north and held in captivity for two years (but not before the elder Scott was maimed by his captors, who removed his thumbs).

Wife and mother Hannah Hawkes Scott was left alone with her father to eke out a living, striving to secure the money needed to ransom her family. Theirs was a family used to the bedevilment of Indians. While living in Deerfield, Hannah's mother, her brother John, his wife and their three children were massacred. A sister, Elizabeth, was captured but died en route to Canada.

The family was finally released after the community scraped together a ransom, but the youngest son chose to remain behind.

Waterbury's answer to this problem, from the start of the colony, was twofold. First, a stockade large enough to include cattle was constructed to encircle the settlement center. Each man was awarded a portion of the fence to maintain. In 1681, the fence was four miles long. By 1709, it had grown to ten miles. It contained four main gates that allowed visitors and outlying inhabitants to enter, and there was an outside pen added to protect stray cattle.

The second portion of the security system the people employed was a continually posted team of sentinels manning two hilltops in Waterbury. The locations provided advantageous views of the valley. Later, after the Scott incident, the watches were increased and a signal system was adopted. No one was excluded from this duty. Waterbury was considered a frontier town in 1710 and was vulnerable to hostile attack.

The General Court in Hartford impressed all persons over age sixteen into the military watch for the defense of their community (excluding blacks and Indians).

Reports of Indian attacks in smaller settlements forced the English to fortify their communities and work together for defense. In Waterbury, there were several incidents that bolstered the fear. Capturing people and holding them for ransom was a practice encouraged by the French since it instilled terror and confusion in the English. The cost stripped the communities financially and forced them into spending valuable time fortifying their towns. The time spent on fortifications was time spent away from the fields, thus placing the crops in jeopardy. Waterbury citizens were required to own arms and have ample supplies of ammunition on hand over and above their needs for hunting. Evenings in Waterbury were spent creating defense strategies at the home of John Stanley, and a small militia was formed of thirty-two men who could muster at a moment's notice.

But the ordeal endured by the Scott family was not the worst. Prior to the attacks, it was the land itself that proved more deadly to the Waterbury community. A great flood in 1691 nearly wiped out the town's crops, and the pestilence that the marshy area encouraged cut deeply into the population.

Despite floods, diseases and hostile natives, the settlements of Connecticut were determined to succeed, and they bolstered the safety of the communities. The General Court sent scouting parties of soldiers to fortify towns. Several forays came through Waterbury and some men from Waterbury followed them. This resulted in a neglect of crops, an oversight Hartford soon assuaged when Waterbury was granted the right to construct its own church in town.

Reverend Jeremiah Peck was the town's first minister to serve in the newly constructed church. His son, Jeremiah Jr., was a carpenter by trade but was knowledgeable enough to serve as the first schoolmaster, first holding classes at his home and later, in 1709, in a rudimentary schoolhouse.

Because of ill health, Reverend Peck served a short time, replaced by the Reverend Southmayd at a salary of fifty pounds a year (mostly paid in produce).

Waterbury persevered and grew. The overriding feature of this community in its earliest stage was the Puritan theocratic nature of its government. School lessons were formed around religious scripture, and laws were stringent with regard to respecting God's dominance over everyone's daily life. Waterbury was a community akin to others throughout New England, tightknit and with a communal purpose. Waterbury does not appear to have had any religious schisms, nor did it contribute to the witchcraft scare that plagued other townships. Members of this community worked diligently to take a foothold for the future and built foundations that let the community grow and prosper.

By 1720, the population was at the eight hundred mark, doubling within the next ten years. By 1774, the number of people doubled again, spread out in an area that included what we call Watertown, Plymouth and other smaller communities. Only one-third of the people lived within the confines of Waterbury's township.

With peace and more inhabitants, the community evolved in two ways. Newcomers brought new ideas and ways with them, and the Puritan community soon found Episcopals within its ranks. The townsfolk expanded their enterprises to include milling and manufacturing, along with agriculture, to sustain the families.

It was a hardscrabble life. Land was more fertile on the outskirts, but for those living in town, the soil and lack of easy passage to other communities made prosperity hard won. A westward migration promised better land for farming, and in the decade beginning in 1810, six hundred people abandoned Waterbury.

Change was inevitable.

In 1775, Waterbury adopted the idea of independence from England and provided 152 soldiers to fight for freedom in what came to be the American Revolution. Historian Charles W. Burpee wrote, "No town in the Colony, not itself the theater of conflict, made greater personal sacrifices throughout the war than Waterbury."

The road passing through Waterbury from east to west had slowly improved and became a strategic route that linked New England with the other states, and it was a route routinely used by marching soldiers and wagon trains. On several occasions, Generals Washington and Lafayette passed through, stopping for food, but the steady stream of soldiers brought trouble by way of smallpox, infecting the community to such a degree that Dr. Abel Bronson established a pesthouse in Middlebury in order to contain the epidemic.

The Revolution brought its own strife within the Waterbury community. The populace was made up of pro-American Puritans, with the small band of Episcopals remaining loyal to the king. The debate was serious enough in Waterbury to ostracize friends and break apart families. The only Tory hanged during this period was a man from Waterbury who had been betrayed by friends and whose father showed no remorse at the hanging.

Moses Dunbar wasn't born in Waterbury, but his family moved to the community in 1760 when Moses was fourteen years old. He was the second of sixteen children in a family that fit into the mores of the Waterbury community.

When he was of age, Moses met and married a young woman from the Farmington community and felt at home with her relations. They were members of the Church of England, a religion Moses adopted as his own.

This defied his own family's beliefs and caused a breach between father and son.

During the early days of the Revolution, as the Continental Congress pondered what action to take against England, Moses was outspoken about his beliefs that secession from the Crown was unlawful. What was agreed upon within his wife's family was not well received in Waterbury, and Moses was soon set upon by a band of forty men and forced to sign a paper of allegiance.

After the unexpected death of his wife, Moses found a local girl to marry and raise his children. He intended to live quietly.

He did not. Because of his views, Moses was deemed a threat and jailed for fourteen days. Upon his release, he left for Long Island to look for land and work where he could live peacefully with other Tory sympathizers.

Finding work proved easier than expected. The Crown was looking for soldiers, and Moses Dunbar was persuaded to enlist men for General Howe, becoming a captain in the British army.

When he returned to Connecticut to collect his family and look for Loyalist recruits, he was betrayed by Joseph Smith and taken into custody at Chippeny Hill in Farmington. With his commission secreted on his person, the local authority sped him off to the larger Farmington community for prosecution. Farmington, in turn, shipped Moses to Hartford, where he was tried on January 23, 1777.

The problem was, Moses hadn't really broken the law. Yet Hartford was going to make an example out of him and, at the same time, demonstrate the state's loyalty to the American cause. Hartford remedied the situation by making Moses's circumstance a crime of high treason punishable by death.

Moses's trial did not last long and the sentence of death was not unexpected. What did surprise those attending was the response of the young man's father when asked if he would plead for leniency for his son. The older man handed over a rope of hemp to be used in the hanging.

When Loyalist Elisha Wadsworth visited Dunbar in prison, he passed a secreted knife to the prisoner. With his bonds cut, Moses Dunbar overpowered his guard temporarily and tried to escape. He was returned to his cell, and Wadsworth was tried for an act that cost him forty pounds and a year in jail.

On March 17, Dunbar's pregnant wife was carted from Waterbury and forced to watch her husband's hanging. Afterward, she made her way to Middletown, to the home of friendly Loyalists who provided her with money with which to care for their four children. Local Patriots drove the poor woman forth under threat of jail.

But for the outcome, Moses Dunbar might have been known as a martyr instead of the only traitor hanged during this conflict.

Moses wasn't the only Waterburian to be arrested for his views. The Reverend Mr. Nichols was likewise arrested but acquitted.

Chapter Two

THE INDUSTRIAL BASE

The American Revolution was political at its core but was launched over economic strife. With independence won, America was put on a path to acquiring wealth from resources that had been steadily siphoned off by England. A great experiment was underway that encouraged growth and achievement, as well as personal freedom. Later, the American Revolution gave way to what was called the Industrial Revolution, and that meant manufacturing on a larger scale.

The Industrial Revolution was born in England and is considered one of the most important events in human history because it changed people's lives. For those of us living today, it is nearly impossible to image what those changes were. Prior to this, most people lived in agrarian communities, often feudal, with wealthy landowners and the Catholic Church controlling the wealth and politics.

The Industrial Revolution had early beginnings. After years of war in Europe and the beginning of a colonization movement, vast changes took place that gradually led to the mechanization of work. The seventeenth century brought forth a scientific revolution that encouraged learning and experimentation. From this, improved methods and product components were developed. Information was exchanged. One result of the exchange of information and changing thought was the Protestant Revolution and the development of a "Protestant" work ethic, which was entrepreneurial by nature.

As a result of the political upheavals in Europe, border controls increased, leading to a diminishing spread of disease, which in turn led to a higher mortality rate for children. Improved agricultural methods improved health overall, and the consequence was a larger, healthier workforce. The stage was set for an Industrial Revolution to begin.

The first step in putting people to work was the cottage industry, particularly weaving and handcrafted items. After James Watt invented the steam engine, more products could be made in less time and in a uniform manner. Later, factories were built to increase efficiency and production. Only a few other inventions caused so drastic a change in the human condition: fire, the wheel, moveable type and the Internet.

According to historian Lewis Mumford, the Industrial Revolution's "archetypal model…was the clock."

Waterbury was well suited for manufacture in its infancy. Plenty of swift-moving water snaked through the town and enabled the settlement to construct its own gristmill, cloth fulling mills and sawmills, all of which made life easier and the town less dependent on other communities. But manufacturing, as we understand it today, began in earnest when Chauncey Jerome began making wooden clocks.

Waterbury didn't invent clocks, but its manufacturers produced fine timepieces that were treasured by the new Americans. The country's citizenry had evolved past the rudimentary dwellings of settlers, and towns were now filled with more comfortable homes that needed to be filled with furniture. Having that furniture made meant that a family could buy more for less, the essential formula for business success. Additionally, home-crafted items could be sold and distributed through the traditional "Yankee Peddler," whose stocked wagons traveled from town to town.

Jerome's early timepieces with wooden gears gave way to brass components, and it was in the manufacture of brass that the city formed the foundation for its future wealth. The making of brass parts for clocks and machinery not only increased output but also standardized the quality of a product, making it more reliable and longer lasting.

The year 1802 was a watershed one for Waterbury's progress when one small water wheel was dedicated to manufacture. James Harrison's shop was an area of only seven by nine feet but it was special. Harrison constructed a log-pipe water system that led to a small, toy-sized water wheel. The one-horsepower wheel aided in the construction of parts for the clocks Harrison manufactured.

Local legend has it that the original brass workers in Waterbury were smuggled out of England in barrels. The story is fanciful but untrue. England had stopped preventing brass workers from emigrating for some time before the brass workers brought their skills to Waterbury.

Among the applications for brass were buttons. Button making became a staple trade in town, creating beautiful adornments that didn't wear out. Nearly one-third of all local manufacturing was engaged in this trade that

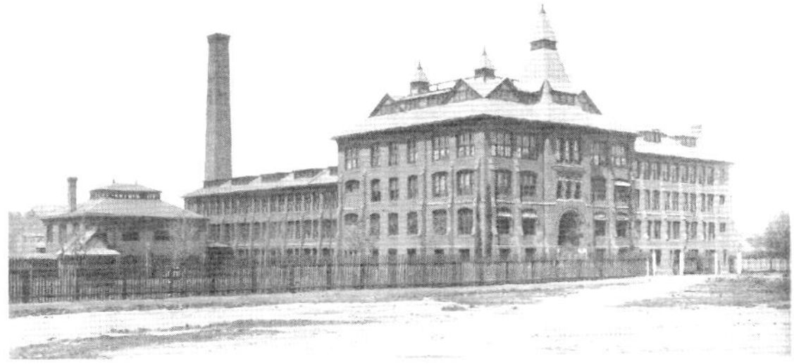

WATERBURY WATCH CO.
While the clock industry may have begun small, Waterbury soon took the lead in creating inexpensive watches for the common man. Reliability was synonymous with "The Waterbury" watch. *From* Waterbury and Her Industries.

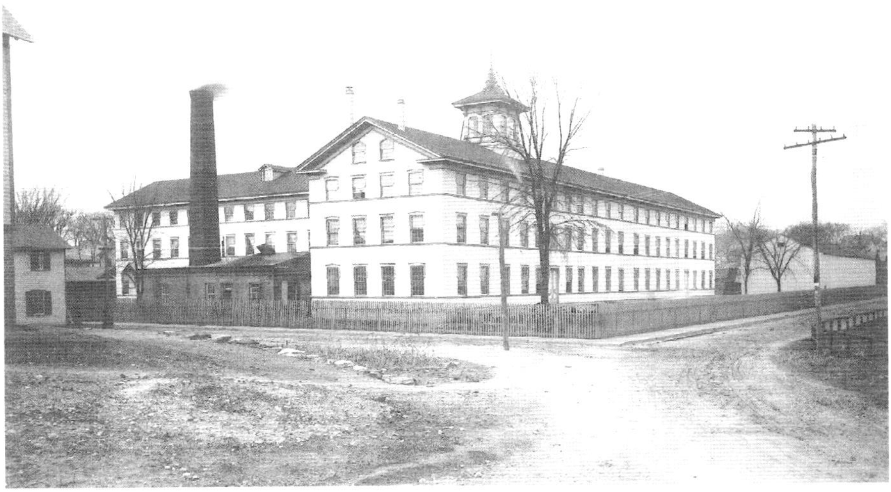

WATERBURY CLOCK CO.
It was the clock that provided Waterbury's first industry. *From* Waterbury and Her Industries.

began in 1750, when Joseph Hopkins, a silversmith, began creating buttons made of enduring metal. Later, the Grilley brothers—Silas, Henry and Samuel—cast pewter buttons on Bunker Hill.

In many ways the true foundation for the brass industry didn't begin in 1802, as history books show, but with the birth of Abel Porter, who served with General Washington and later lived in Southington, where he worked as a tinner. Abel earned a fortune with his factory, which employed five men, and he invested in land, some of it in Waterbury.

It was in Waterbury where he met Daniel Clark and learned of the growing button trade. Abel saw that his experience and money could be advantageous for him, and so a partnership agreement was drawn up by Abel that named his brother Levi, Clark and Silas Grilley as partners. The year was 1802 and Abel was forty-five years old. Abel and Levi contributed their skills at button making, capital and equipment. Grilley had skill at crafting single-eye pewter buttons, and Clark had connections that would later lead them to acquiring the Hopkins Grist Mill on the Mad River. In 1804, the partnership expanded to include button maker David Hayden of Attleboro, Massachusetts.

Early businessmen suffered from lack of capital. The mortality rate was high and banks did not see small manufacturers as good risks. Small loans from more successful businessmen and partnerships were most often the key to growth for entrepreneurs. Securing a partner with experience and fortune was the wisest move and explains why so many men in Waterbury found themselves involved in a multitude of businesses.

The Porter partnership was forged at a time when the industry was changing away from soft metal buttons made of pewter to harder metals that could be made from the scraps of old metalware.

The inconsistency inherent in producing metal from scrap was a problem that the men solved by casting and cold rolling brass strips, metal made by alloying copper with zinc. This process, invented by Englishman James Emerson in 1781, required more water and hotter fires.

The partners lacked mill power but employed a bellows to raise temperatures, using horse-, man- or boy power. In 1808, the problem was solved when the Hopkins Grist Mill was acquired. At this juncture the partnership was re-formed. Levi Porter sold his shares to David Hayden. Silas Grilley left. Abel Porter, in turn, bought out Hayden and Clark, selling the entire enterprise to Frederick Leavenworth, James Scovill and his son James Mitchell Lamson Scovill.

In time, the elder Scovill sold his shares to young James. Hayden was retained as an employee until 1814, when he again acquired a partnership stake. With this combination, the company was poised to grow. Scovill provided sales and management skills, while Leavenworth and Hayden tended to the manufacturing processes.

The company's next improvement came with the hiring of English immigrant James Croft, who returned to his native country to recruit brass workers and learn the latest rolling and casting techniques.

The younger brother of J.M.L. Scovill, William Henry, joined the company, replacing Leavenworth and Hayden. The company was renamed J.M.L. & W.H. Scovill until it finally became Scovill Manufacturing Company in 1850.

The basic process of brass production in Waterbury was to melt copper and zinc, pouring the mix into molds to form metal bars. The bars were then alternately rolled to compress the metal and annealed (heated and

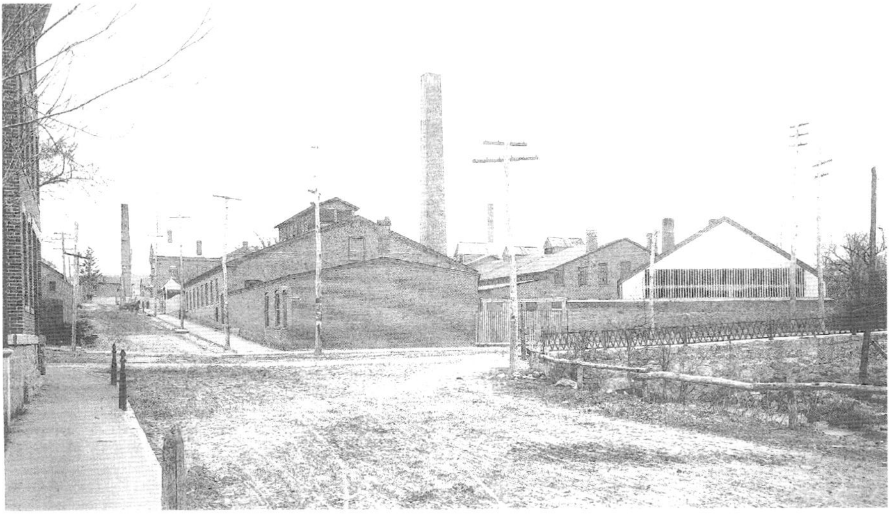

Scovill Co.
The Scovill brothers forged a giant industry along the Mad River. Its wartime production was prolific, and future leaders would include the Goss brothers and Malcolm Baldridge. *From* Waterbury and Her Industries.

then cooled) to soften the brass into a certain thickness. The beginning of brass manufacturing supplied heat from charcoal pits and bellows. By 1830, charcoal was replaced with anthracite coal until the twentieth century, when oil-fired furnaces and, later, induction furnaces were employed.

Companies like Scovill didn't succeed by sticking to one product, and the company was always looking for niches to fill. After spending decades manufacturing buttons, fasteners and other hardware, the company embraced the invention of the daguerreotype when it was invented in 1839. Scovill first developed the silver-coated copper sheets—and, later, tin sheets—as well as manufacturing a multitude of camera parts and photographic equipment. Until 1874, it was a lucrative portion of the business, but technical changes in photography were moving it away from metals. Scovill then decided to drop that portion of its operation.

A part of the photography division was creating decorative cases to house the photographs. Samuel Peck of New Haven had developed a mix of gum shellac and wood fibers to form a plastic material. The plastic was heated and molded at Scovill and distributed across the world. The company had acquired the rights to plastic before Peck's company folded, and in 1883 the process was brought to Waterbury.

The size and scope of Scovill Manufacturing was enormous and had a great impact on the community; oftentimes it seemed to be a town within itself, with its own newspaper, clubs, a library, a cafeteria and even a sunshine fund. It also held a "factory town" grip on its employees, registering those who participated in strikes and noting marital status, literacy rates, et cetera.

Scovill wasn't the only brass manufacturer in what became known as the Brass Capital of the World. Others were making their way into the industry, oftentimes with employees and partners with close connections to competitors. The shift from small factories to industrial giants that took place around 1850 made some of the manufacturers look to the future and how competition could hurt them.

In 1853, the American Brass Association was formed to oversee pricing and regulate production. This voluntary cooperative of companies re-formed in 1899 as the American Brass Company with the merging of the Coe Brass Company of Torrington, the Waterbury Brass Company and the Ansonia Brass and Copper Co. The following year, Benedict & Burnham Manufacturing Company joined the group, followed by Holmes, Booth & Haydens in 1902. By 1912, this "holding company" changed to an operating company, thus making it what author Isaac Marcosson termed "the largest fabricator of non-ferrous metals in brass, and the largest fabricator of non-ferrous metals in the world."

The buttons were also a connection to the military for the town. Aside from sending soldiers to fight for freedom, Waterbury's button manufacturers provided gleaming brass buttons for uniforms, a link that continued through the Civil War, two world wars and beyond. Later, artillery shell casings made of brass, nautical equipment and bomb fuses became wartime staples.

And so, before the high point of the Industrial Revolution truly got started in 1850, Waterbury had formed a solid manufacturing base that quickly replaced agriculture. Entrepreneurial young men began their trades humbly, erecting rude buildings along the watercourses. During the warmer months water powered the mills, and in the winter horses were employed. Large families often had children who could work. When enough capital was built, employers could invest in better machinery and in more permanent and efficient buildings.

Several individuals stand out in Waterbury's clock manufacturing history. Following Chauncey Jerome's lead, Eli Terry and his sons established their own clock-making facility and quickly became known for their craftsmanship. Soon the demand for their clocks exceeded their ability to produce, and so Eli Terry sold his original company to his apprentice, Herman Clark. The Terrys then bought an existing business two miles north of Waterville in order to fulfill a contract: producing four thousand clocks within three years. When the contract ended in 1810, Terry sold his factory to Seth Thomas and Silas Hoadley.

Notable Transcendentalist A. Bronson Alcott wrote about the clock trade, harkening back to his own apprenticeship while growing up in the Waterbury area. His work *New Connecticut* refers to the twelve months he spent working as a clockmaker, a time when he fitted clock parts together for many hours during the day. The dull, dreary work left him no time to study. Alcott's teachings were a direct response to the industrialization he witnessed all around him, and his influence was passed on to his daughter, notable American author Louisa May Alcott.

The burgeoning brass industry and the clock-making enterprises in town converged when brass became a staple part of making timepieces. Brass allowed for the manufacture of smaller, reliable watches, and the goal of Waterbury's industrial barons was to create a watch inexpensive enough that everyone in the country could afford to own one. Later, Robert Ingersoll's one-dollar pocket watch sold to five million people, and it was estimated that nearly fifteen hundred per day were produced. "The Waterbury," as the watch was dubbed, was so ingrained in the mind of the public that it shows up in literature as a symbol of reliability.

Goals such as this spurred steady growth in Waterbury. The city was not alone. America was filling with people and expanding into new territories. This meant that products were needed on an ever-growing basis. More people traveling meant more carts, more means of transportation. More homes filled with furniture, fixtures and decorations was a demand that didn't seem to stop. And this, in turn, seemed to create an epidemic of brick factories sprouting up everywhere as the nineteenth century reached its midpoint.

One family's story brings this period of growth into focus. The Platts came to Connecticut with the New Haven colony in 1639 and had five generations of farmers, moving first to Milford, then to Waterbury and finally to Newtown, always in search of cheaper land for their expanding family. During their brief stay in Waterbury, the land they acquired was lent to the Congregational Church, a gesture that brought later rewards.

In the 1790s, Connecticut was a populated state, and farmers were in constant need of larger homesteads. A great exodus began, siphoning off agricultural workers to Vermont, New Hampshire, western New York, Pennsylvania and the Western Reserve (Ohio).

Nathan Platt was a member of the third generation of Platts living in Newtown and bucked this trend. He returned to Waterbury at the behest of his friend Mark Leavenworth, whose grandfather was the Congregationalist minister who had benefited from the Platt family largesse. Leavenworth urged Platt to go into manufacturing, as he had done, making buckles and clocks. He pointed to the plethora of water sources and the power water could deliver and assured the young farmer that manufacturing was the way to future wealth.

At that time, Lemuel Hoadley bought a mill and created dams with races that allowed him to construct a sawmill, a gristmill, a flax-breaking mill and a nail works. Of this mix, one can see the subtle change from the agricultural base of commerce to the manufacturing method. The sawmill and gristmill were entirely connected to an agrarian economy. The flax mill took the place of a heretofore cottage industry, and the nail works was entirely manufacturing.

The nail works was taken over by Jesse Hopkins, who teamed up with Jared Byington. Together they learned to slit metal to produce nails on the grain, as opposed to the traditional method used by ironworkers to individually cut across the grain. The machine that the pair fashioned increased production fivefold and expanded the market outward so as not to flood the local area with cheap products. They petitioned the state for a $5,000 no-interest loan and provided a customer's affidavit to show that the products worked well.

The state denied the grant, and the two had to capitalize their company with land sales. Hopkins sold the land holding the nail works to Platt in 1797 but still needed $1,700 to fully fund his venture. Local merchant Aaron Benedict Sr. loaned him the sum. Matthew Roth, author of *Platt Brothers and Company*, noted that "general store merchants were the only people in rural Connecticut who could finance small manufacturers."

The local economy until then had relied on farmers helping farmers, and all goods were sold through merchants. Thus, merchants had access to money from all households. By helping manufacturers, the merchant would have more goods to sell.

Slowly the manufacturing economy would expand beyond the local limits and bring goods to metropolitan areas like New York, where salesmen would supplant the Yankee Peddlers by traveling through the country selling goods made by Waterbury factories.

Young manufacturing concerns were often cobbled together with investments and partnerships made up of local businessmen and residents. As partnership agreements reached their ends, some would drop out as partnership fees rose.

Despite the good idea and superior product, Hopkins was short on cash and defaulted on his loan from Benedict. Platt invested his mother's inheritance by paying off the loan to Benedict and gained ownership of the nail works, along with full control of the water rights. He then embarked on paying off all his outstanding debts and educating his children.

Money made was used to buy land along the Naugatuck River, in a section that became known as Platts Mills. Platt bought water rights and established manufacturing facilities to complement his farms.

Nathan Platt's son Alfred took control of the company and broke tradition by becoming a member of the Baptist Church, a sect that broke from the state-sanctioned Congregationalist Church. His success in business afforded him the honor of being one of four area businessmen pledging funds for the construction of a Greek Revival–style church on South Main Street. The money would be defrayed by the pledges of the church's other parishioners.

All went well until the Panic of 1837. The national economic contraction created a shortage of cash. The Silliman brothers, who built the new church, saw that the church members could no longer afford to help defray costs and placed a lien against the four guarantors. An assessment of $900 was placed against Alfred Platt.

The panic collapsed the banking system, and money coming into Waterbury from out of state dried up. Platt was reduced to borrowing money from friends to pay his taxes and other obligations.

The aftermath of this panic was growth, and the value of Platt's land rose. He persevered, knowing that the farm would feed his entire family of six sons. All worked to produce the food, with the women contributing fully. The gristmill and sawmill provided income to sustain the family. Metalworking was their investment for the future.

Of his sons, only one did not live at home. Nirom and his wife lived next door. Nirom became a businessman, owning a shop, and another son, Seabury, became a lawyer.

The year 1850 was a pivotal one for the Platts and Waterbury as a whole. The town had seen agriculture decline and the population swell to five thousand, with one thousand of those being Irish who immigrated to new jobs to avoid the Great Famine.

The Platts were well placed in Waterbury. They had secured land and water rights and had solid business ties to other manufacturing concerns in town. Their world was changing around them as the farmland changed to work yards. Waterbury was developing a pattern for growth and change. Factories were constructed everywhere and stores opened throughout the community. Transport companies were formed and hotels were erected. Builders were in high demand.

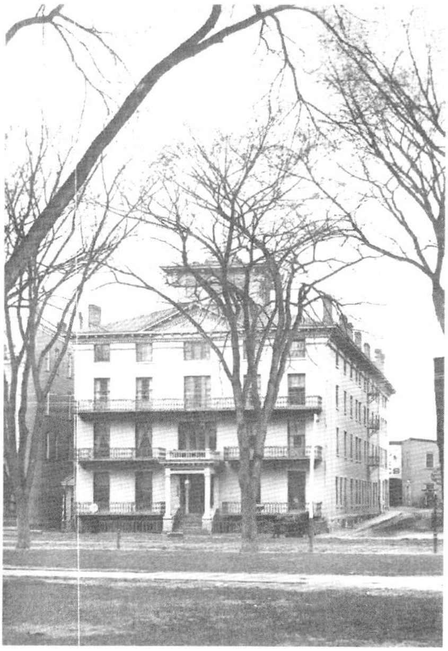

Scovill House
Scovill House was a sign of progress. There was enough business in Waterbury to warrant a first-class hotel. *From* Waterbury and Her Industries.

Green Kendrick pushed local industrialists to invest in the Naugatuck Railroad in 1849, and the Platts saw the rail line constructed by Irish immigrants across the river from their property. For them, the nearest depot was one mile south in Union City, where their goods would be taken by train to Derby's steamships.

Alfred Platt knew his place "in the food chain" of this period and did not compete directly with the larger metal industries, nor did he produce products in direct competition with his neighbors. The niche Platt developed was with zinc, a metal deemed hard to work with, but by 1847 the family had learned enough to construct a method for rolling zinc.

Alfred defied local sympathies and welcomed the new Irish workers, even boarding one young man named Daniel Bergan in his home.

Among the companies the Platts had as "neighbors," there was the American Ring Co. of Waterbury, founded in 1852, which provided home trimmings for umbrellas, doors, suspender rings, sleigh bells and harness ornaments.

A demand for buttons during the Civil War changed the upward swing of business in a contradictory sense—it made raw materials scarce and expensive and put labor more in demand. It also made machinery more available and created a great demand for buttons. The Platts quickly capitalized on this need, providing buttons to the military, not only for uniforms but also for tents. Roth writes, "The wartime demand enriched the Platts."

Despite a drop in postwar demand for buttons, the price of goods plummeted. The Platt family took their earnings and invested in raw materials, a wise move because it didn't take long for civilian orders to rise and the manufacturing field had fewer competitors.

When Alfred died, the sons took over the business, and throughout the remainder of the nineteenth century they worked to expand the enterprise in production and in location, by moving some of its manufacturing sites toward downtown. To fully guarantee that the family's interests were maintained, the Platts did what was then quite innovative—they appointed two women (Carrie Platt and Helen Camp) as directors.

The production of brass was the mainstay, and the rolling mills sprawled over vast tracts of land within the city's borders. The products were diverse and often cutting edge. The photographs of factories used in this book were originally shot with a Scovill-developed camera and process and were originally printed in the book *Waterbury and Her Industries*. The Platts were at the heart of it all.

Waterbury was a town in motion by 1850, a year some writers call the beginning of Waterbury's Golden Age. On nearly every street in the central portion of the city where the waters converged, factories were being erected, brick by brick, story by story. Blocks of land were covered, and the dirt roads were packed hard with the hooves of horses bringing materials.

When the demand for labor exceeded the population, immigrants were encouraged to come and settle, in Waterbury and all other major cities across the country. Hundreds were employed in each of the many factories and were paid in script that was redeemable in company stores.

Those original inhabitants of Waterbury who turned to manufacturing grew wealthy. Large, stately homes were erected throughout the town, and soon more ornate churches, lively entertainments and better schools ensued. With the pleasures that wealth brought, these citizens also felt a responsibility for building their community.

One of the key aspects to Waterbury's growth was the railroad that ran through the factory yards and stopped at the Waterbury station on Meadow Street. Along with freight, the railroad also provided the wealthy with access to metropolitan regions like New York for both business and pleasure. Early railroads in Waterbury offered the same connections to the country that the roads had during the Revolution. The rail lines ran north to south, with Waterbury as a hub between Winsted and Bridgeport. Those rails running east to west connected Hartford and Danbury to the Brass City.

If one were to scrutinize Waterbury's success with brass and try to duplicate it today, it would be impossible. The raw materials needed for production were not found locally, and it all had to be shipped in from elsewhere. Labor costs would be astronomical compared to the meager wages and scripts early laborers received.

The beginnings of a true industrial base began in town in earnest when Benedict and Burnham opened its doors in 1812 with $6,500 in capital. By 1885, the company had grown in partnership, adding Israel Coe in 1829, and in the number of workers, with eight hundred employees.

The large company periodically broke into parts, spawning more focused enterprises like the Waterbury Button Company, the Waterbury Clock Company, the American Pin Company and the Waterbury Watch Company. The articles produced here included gilded metal, brass tubing, wire, buttons, pins, knobs, safety pins, rivets, hinges, printers' rules, galley plates, oil burners, lamp trip and many other household items.

It happened within every local company, according to Roth:

> *Waterbury's Big 5 (the brass mills) controlled more than half of the nation's market for primary brass products (sheet, tube, wire) in the 1880's; with the four other major producers from the Naugatuck Valley and Bridgeport, the immediate region accounted for some 76% of the national output. These nine firms constituted the American Brass Association which had been established in 1853 as the mechanism for agreements on pricing and production limits.*

When smaller companies faced obstacles, larger ones bought them out. The Platts, however, did not want to be acquired. At the end of the nineteenth century, the family had Platts Mills along the Naugatuck and the Patent Button Company downtown. The second company was most vulnerable to a takeover. Company president Thomas Porter advised the family to acquire firms that posed threats or to license their patents in order to hold their dominant position. Alfred's son Clark felt that adhering to the family's principle of success through innovation and creating a superior product was their armor. It became a debate between acquisitions and product change. But when Clark died suddenly, Porter pushed his position, and in 1901 it was the only independent button maker to survive intact.

The Platt Brothers gristmill caught fire in 1895, leaving it with additional land to expand its manufacturing enterprise. Roth writes, "When the Platt Brothers consolidated all of the Platts Mills water rights, it also acquired the legal standing to address the enormous health problem resulting from the pollution of the Naugatuck River."

With so much growth in manufacturing, the Naugatuck River had indeed become polluted. During the years between 1884 and 1889, Waterbury constructed a sewer system that helped alleviate typhus, cholera and dysentery. The sewage was collected and dumped into the Naugatuck River, flowing downstream past the Platt factories and homes. Their response was to sue the city, claiming that the river had become a conduit of filth that fouled the Platt property.

The claim was that vile and noxious odors and filthy water made the factories and homes downstream unwholesome and adversely affected their ability to do business. The city responded with the excuse that it did not create the sewage; the city merely collected it. Therefore, the Platts must sue the people and factories that created the waste. The city hoped that this rejoinder would pit the local manufacturers against the Platts, but the tactic failed.

The city then argued that since the Platt factory near to downtown contributed to the sewage system, the Platts were suing themselves. That argument, too, was denounced.

The final argument the city put forth was that the sewage added to the river increased the water flow, thereby making the river more valuable for Platts Mills. And, after all, the city had no choice but to foul the river. What could be done?

The answer took another three-quarters of a century.

In 1898, the Superior Court agreed with the Platts, and the appeal filed in 1903 upheld this decision, forcing the city to install filters and dump sewage only during summer months. Waterbury was obliged to pay the Platts $2,800 a year as a penalty.

The penalty was finally quit when, in 1952, the city's health department mandated that a sewage treatment plant be built.

This put the Platts in the position of being the first environmentalist activists in town and changing the way the public viewed the river. Until their case, the river was seen as something to be used freely by anyone, regardless of the effect it had on others downstream. The Platt suit laid the groundwork for pollution being linked to responsible parties.

Thus began another turning point in the city's development.

The only hindrance to this unprecedented growth was the transportation routes that allowed for goods to be brought into town and products to leave it. In the earliest days, the roads leading into and out of Waterbury were dirt traces that, over time, widened into lanes connecting to Danbury, Hartford and New Haven. Early manufacturers relied on the peddler trade to disperse goods, but the peddlers were often unreliable means. Traveling to and from any of the three nearby towns would cost a day's time.

Chapter Three

THE CIVIL WAR

The boon in business and invention was temporarily breached by the Civil War. It affected every state and placed demands on factories for munitions. Waterbury responded with goods, but the city's true participation in the Civil War can be illustrated by one man's honor, Colonel John Lyman Chatfield, who was born in Oxford in 1826 and moved to the city as a young man of twenty-five.

Chatfield's earliest military training came locally with the Derby Blues, and in 1854 he raised a unit of men for the Waterbury City Guard and became its captain. Following the fall of Fort Sumter, President Lincoln called for three-month volunteers for the War Between the States, and the Waterbury Guard traveled to New Haven to train with Company D of the First Connecticut Volunteer Infantry. Chatfield quickly earned promotions, first to major and later to colonel.

This marked a turning point for local militiamen. After having provided soldiers for the Revolution, the War of 1812 and the War with Mexico, the long peace eroded a sense of discipline that led to the company being dubbed with the derisive name "Flood Woods." Attempts were made by Hartford to find a company leader who could bring the group into a tighter discipline. Chatfield, as a result, had to begin anew and construct a fighting group that would serve with honor.

Chatfield and the other volunteers began their three-month tour of duty in Washington, D.C., at a time when Rebel flags were visible from Capitol Hill. He was dispatched to the Third Connecticut Regiment in Virginia and was engaged in battle by August 1, after which he was commended for his courage under fire.

The Connecticut Volunteers were mustered out, but Chatfield quickly reenlisted for a three-year term of service and raised a regiment, becoming colonel of the Connecticut Sixth Regiment. The hard work spent training taxed Chatfield's health, and he was forced to convalesce until rejoining his men in January 1862, leading the attack on Fort Pulaski and the other fortifications guarding Savannah, Georgia.

By October of that year, Chatfield was employed to lead a brigade, taking over from a previous leader who had been deemed incompetent. Chatfield refused the rank of brigadier general, choosing to remain a colonel and stay with the men of the Sixth Connecticut.

His assignment was to destroy all lines of communication between Savannah and Charleston, and during the campaign against Pocotaligo, he was wounded by canister shot. With an injured leg, the colonel was forced to crawl to safety through snake-infested terrain.

The Sixth Connecticut regained its leader in April 1863, and the following July Chatfield joined other Northern forces in an attack on the southeast end of Morris Island. The early victory they gained was not swiftly followed up and the lag cost the troops dearly. General Gillmore soon saw the wisdom of launching a bombardment before sending in his men.

From noon to twilight, projectiles began firing at the fort before the "Glory Assault" began. The Sixth Connecticut was directly behind the Massachusetts Fifty-fourth Regiment led by Colonel Robert Gould Shaw. Shaw commandeered an all-black volunteer company, which broke the tradition of the law of 1792 barring Negroes from bearing arms in the U.S. military, despite their tradition of participating in the American Revolution.

Lincoln's heavy losses loosened this restriction, and the Fifty-fourth Regiment was the country's first all–African American regiment. Their story is immortalized in the movie *Glory*.

As the Fifty-fourth approached Fort Wagner, Colonel Shaw was killed, leaving the regiment temporarily disorganized. Colonel Chatfield and the Sixth Connecticut pushed the Fifty-fourth and their own company forward to the moat of Fort Wagner and breached the fort, fighting hand to hand amid the dense smoke and bullet fire.

The Fifty-fourth valiantly secured a portion within the fort, and cries of victory arose throughout the enclave, but when the troops outside the fort lost cohesion, the Fifty-fourth and Sixth were unsupported during a battle that raged for three hours.

At one point during the battle, Chatfield saw Color Sergeant Gustave de Bouge of Waterbury shot in the head. The banner he carried was covered in blood and captured by a Rebel soldier. Soon Chatfield himself was shot in the leg, and again in the hand, nearly severing it and shattering his ornamental sword. With no relief coming, he ordered a man-by-man retreat from the fort, slowly making his own way to safety.

As a testament to the regard with which his men valued their leader, Private Bernard Haffey of the G Company lay down beside Chatfield as the colonel withdrew and provided a human shield from the fray. Private Grogan of Bridgeport helped lead Chatfield to safety, after which the colonel was returned to his home state aboard the steamship *Arago*.

Arriving in Waterbury on July 31, Chatfield repaired to bed as his wounds worsened. After refusing the amputation of his leg, the hero died on August 9, 1863. The city publicly mourned its fallen son and city business was halted. The flags were lowered to half staff, and public buildings were adorned with black crêpe. Dignitaries filled St. John's on the Green for Chatfield's funeral, and the cortege winding its way to Riverside Cemetery was accorded the respect of tolling bells and shots fired.

In honor of Chatfield, the Waterbury Company was named the Chatfield Guard when the state militia was renamed the Connecticut National Guard. To honor all of Waterbury's military participants in the Civil War, a monument was erected in 1884, and the dedication in October was attended by as many as thirty thousand people.

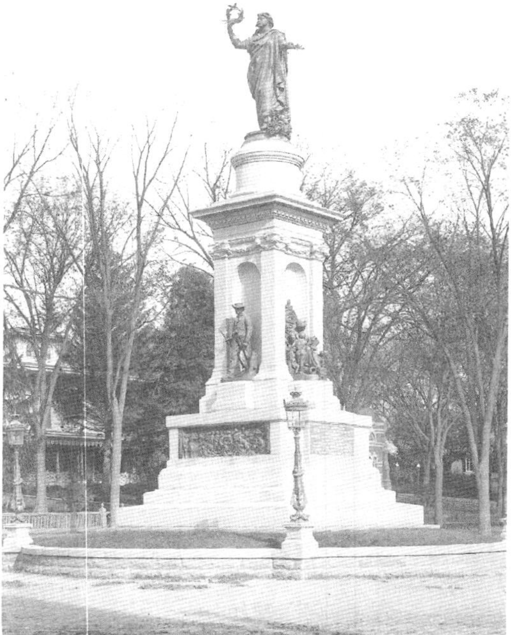

Soldiers' Monument
George Bissell's design contained realistic sculptures that represented more than the fighting man. The artist wanted to incorporate the philosophy behind the Civil War. *From* Waterbury and Her Industries.

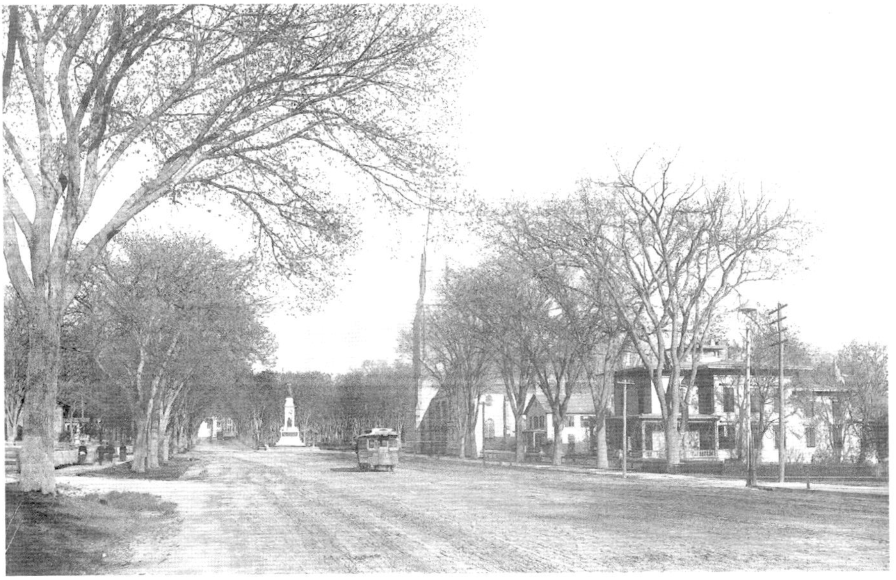

West Main Street
The Soldiers' Monument was the focal point for those traveling west on West Main Street (on the north side of the green). *From* Waterbury and Her Industries.

The monument was designed by George Bissell and depicts realistic figures on a granite pedestal. Originally planned for the center of the green, the monument was finally placed at the western end, next to St. John's Church, and with that decision, the original height of sixty feet was shortened to forty-eight so as not to compete with the church's steeple.

The monument was commissioned by the city with funds of more than $23,000 contributed by 1,150 individuals. The design was bold for its day. Rather than relying on allegorical figures, Bissell used realistic images and incorporated the theme of emancipation and educating African Americans.

Several years later, in 1888, another Bissell statue was unveiled. It was a twelve-foot-high grave marker of a Civil War leader atop a granite pedestal. Though it is surmised that the likeness isn't Chatfield's, it was commissioned by Chatfield's friends to commemorate the fallen hero.

Chapter Four

CALAMITIES

The first snowstorm of great magnitude in Waterbury was recorded in 1798. Two more struck the city in ninety-year intervals. The second major blizzard arrived on Sunday, March 11, 1888, a day that had been mild, with temperatures reaching into the forties. The storm roared in just after midnight, with high winds and tremendous snows that drifted up to twelve feet over roads and railroad tracks, stranding passengers en route. The storm continued until Tuesday noon, and in the end fifty inches of snow had fallen in forty-eight hours.

The heavy snowfall paralyzed train traffic along the shore for eight days and stranded passengers overnight on the trains running to and from Waterbury. The New York & New Haven rail line reported more than a dozen engines disabled and thirty-eight freight and passenger trains stranded.

Newspapers were filled with tales of passengers "making do" with makeshift beds while trying to keep up their spirits. In the rail car called the Derby, several passengers huddled together to sleep.

The car was cold and the wind was howling. Snow flew sideways past the window. As the passengers drifted off to sleep, the cries of a cat were heard. It was a plaintive cry, and the passengers' hearts felt for the stranded cat. A search commenced, with some passengers leaning out the door crying, "Here kitty!"

Along the track and under the car no paw prints were found. Soon the cat was heard no more, and the people shook off the snow from their coats and settled down to sleep.

"Meow," the beast was heard crying. "Meow, meow!"

Again a search resulted in no cat.

"Meow," one of the passengers said, laughing. Never before had the hobby of ventriloquism been more fun.

In another car down the line a group of friends was resting. Soon a snorting sound drowned out the wind. The snoring man's friends crept close and slid matchsticks into his beard. "Light it," one friend goaded the other. Slowly and carefully the matches were ignited.

"Fire," everyone shouted and laughed as the sleeping man jumped to the floor, beating out the flames surrounding his face.

For some, the storm proved more tiresome. After one locomotive ran out of water during the storm, it was towed to Beacon Falls once the track was clear. Here a path had been dug, leading from the tracks to the river. Railroad employees and passengers alike formed a bucket brigade to haul twenty-seven hundred pails full of river water to the engine.

The cleanup began as teams of workers hit the streets, shoveling paths along the sidewalks. It didn't take long for shutterbugs to set up cameras to capture the scenes of the Great Blizzard.

In Waterbury, snow piles along the downtown curbs reached well over a man's head, and one scene of Bank Street showed the snow blanketing the street to be half a story high.

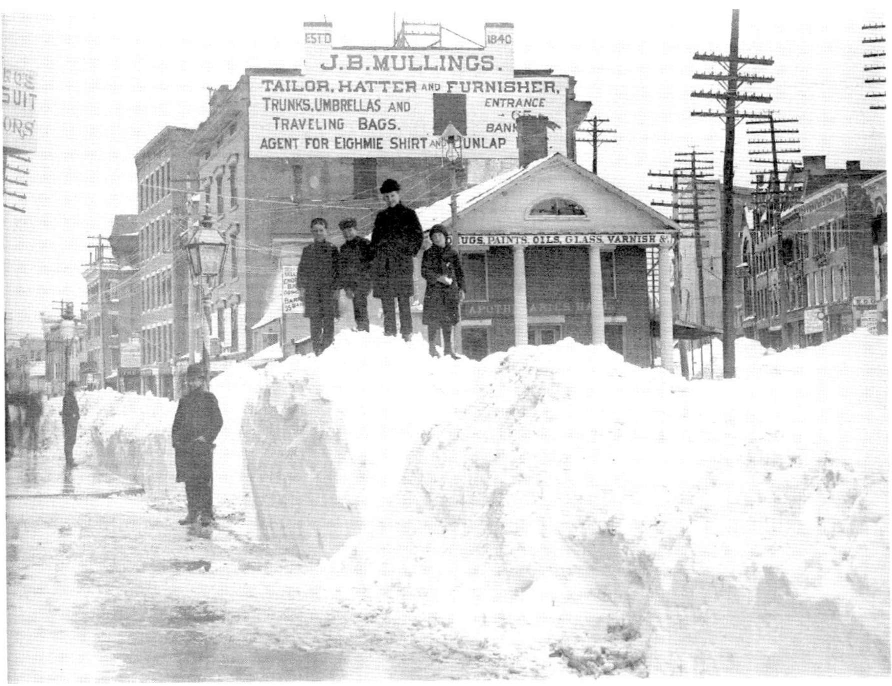

Great Blizzard

The scene at Exchange Place clearly demonstrates the power of the Great Blizzard. Trains were stranded for days, and cities came to a standstill until the roads and sidewalks could be cleared. *From the author's collection.*

It wasn't until 1978 when another nor'easter crippled the state and southern New England. Fifty-five inches of snow fell from February 5 to 8. The snow came quickly and workers took to the highways. The speed with which it hit caught everyone by surprise and many found themselves stranded. Massachusetts reported that some people trapped in running cars were asphyxiated when snow covered their tailpipes.

Governor Ella Grasso closed the state to give the National Guard, city and state workers time to clear the roads. The number of abandoned cars that littered the streets made that task nearly impossible.

In the Robinwood section of Waterbury, people took to skis and snowmobiles. Once things returned to normal, children walking to school were all but invisible behind snow banks.

Snow wasn't the only form of precipitation to plague Waterbury. The first recorded flood happened in 1691, but it wasn't until 1896 that another flood would stand out. It happened in early February and caused thousands of dollars in damages, filling the green with one to three feet of water. On the Naugatuck River, bridges above and below the town were swept away.

A few years later, fire changed the face of Waterbury's downtown.

February 2, 1902, was a day of cold drizzle, with high winds expected overnight. At 6:15 p.m., A.L. Lyall, E.T. Crooker and A.K. Burnham left

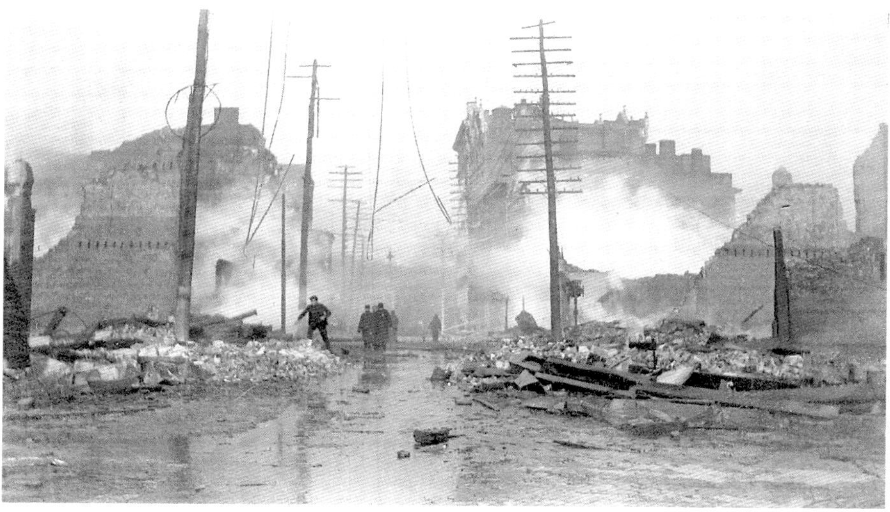

Fire, Bank Street North

The fire swept through town, beginning on Bank Street. This is the view looking north. *From the author's collection.*

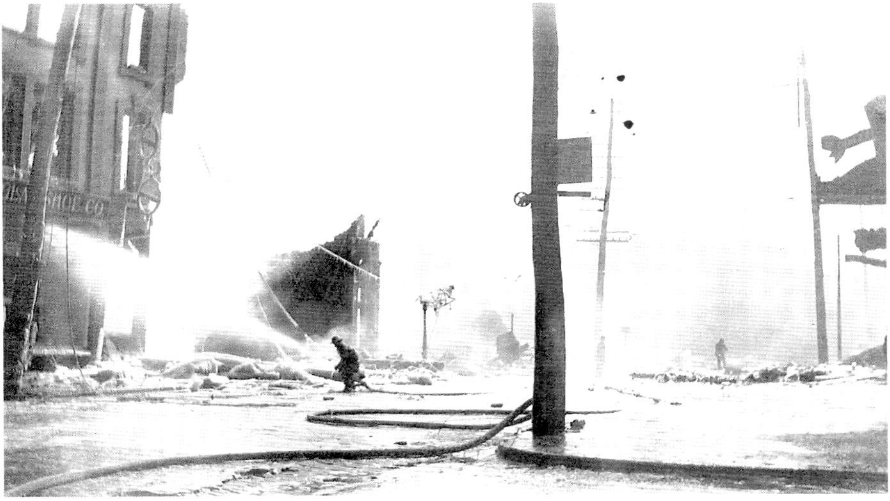

FIRE, CENTER STREET
Center Street is where the firefighters hoped to stop the spread of the blaze. *From the author's collection.*

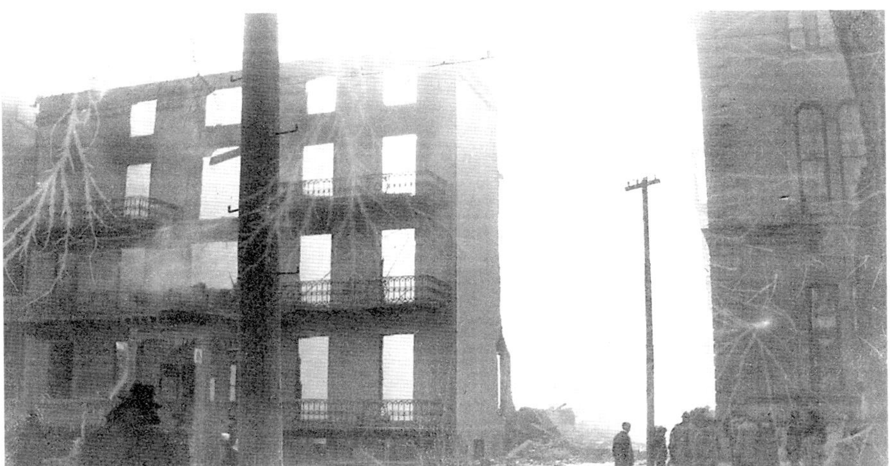

TENEMENTS ON FIRE
Downtown was filled with tenement apartments. After the fire, more than thirty families were homeless. *From the author's collection.*

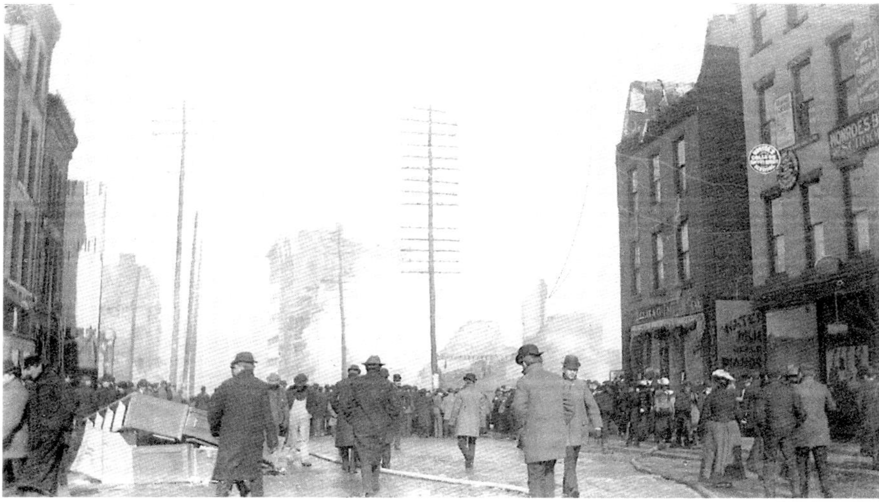

Fire, Bank Street
People flocked to the scene on Bank Street to witness the unthinkable. *From the author's collection.*

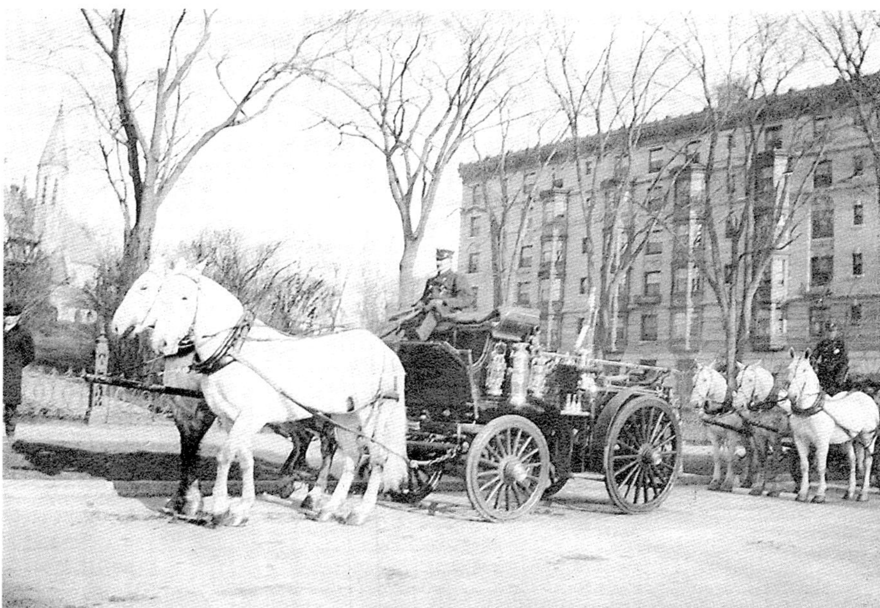

Fire Engine with Horses
Engine companies responded from throughout the region. The equipment used to fight Waterbury's biggest fire was primitive by today's standards. *From the author's collection.*

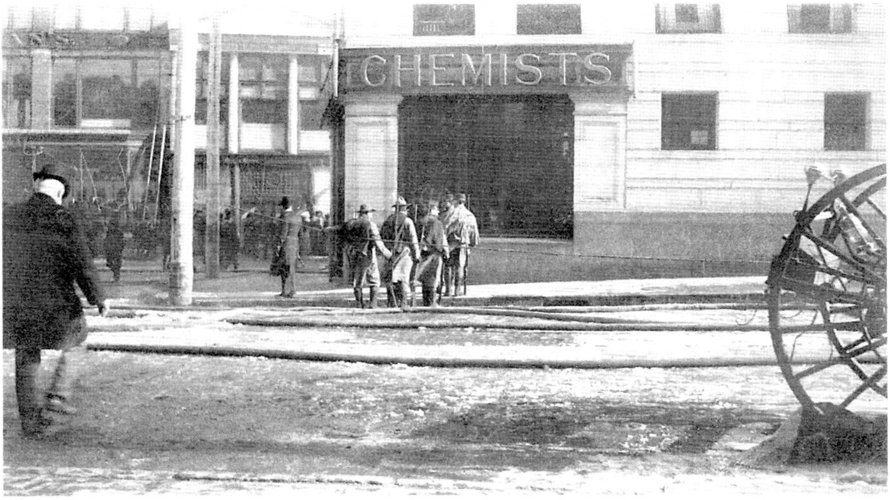

FIRE HOSES AND MILITIA
Water was pumped over the smoldering ruins to prevent new fires. This photo was taken on Bank Street at Apothecaries Hall. *From the author's collection.*

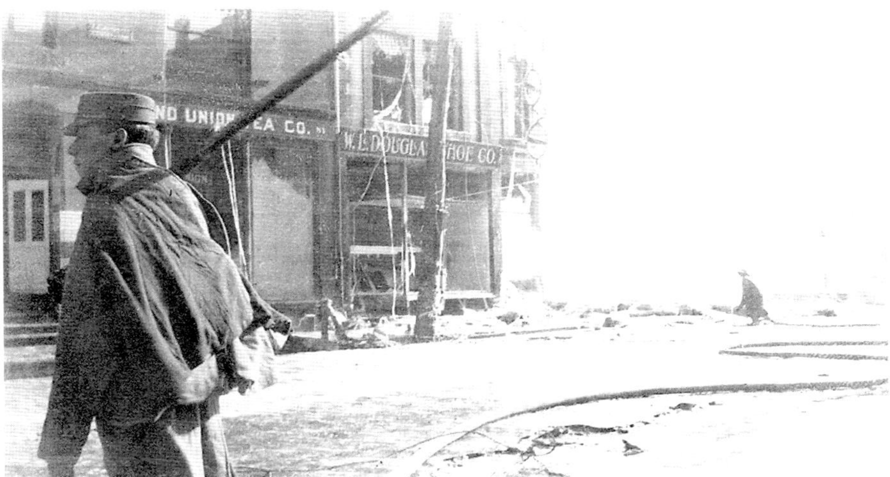

MILITIA MAN AT FIRE
The state National Guard patrolled the streets to prevent looting and to provide order. In 1902, the uniform was more similar to those worn during the Civil War than to those of today. *From the author's collection.*

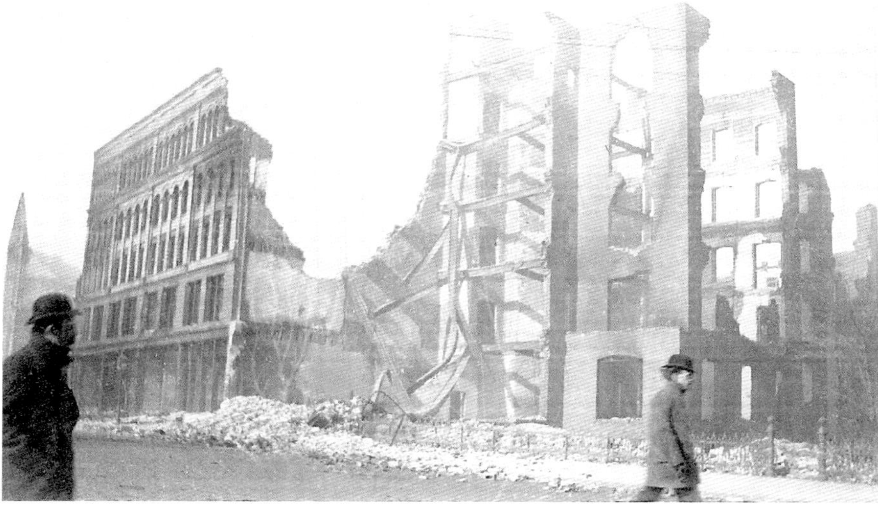

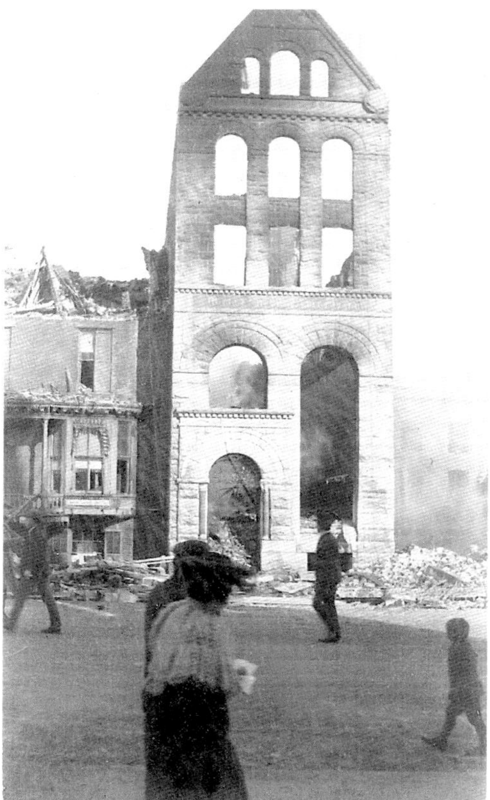

Above: New England Engineering Building
The New England Engineering building was little more than a shell after the fire was quelled. *From the author's collection.*

Left: American Building Façade
The granite front of the American newspaper building was what remained of Grand Street from Leavenworth to Bank. This was the only structure to retain a portion of the original building. *From the author's collection.*

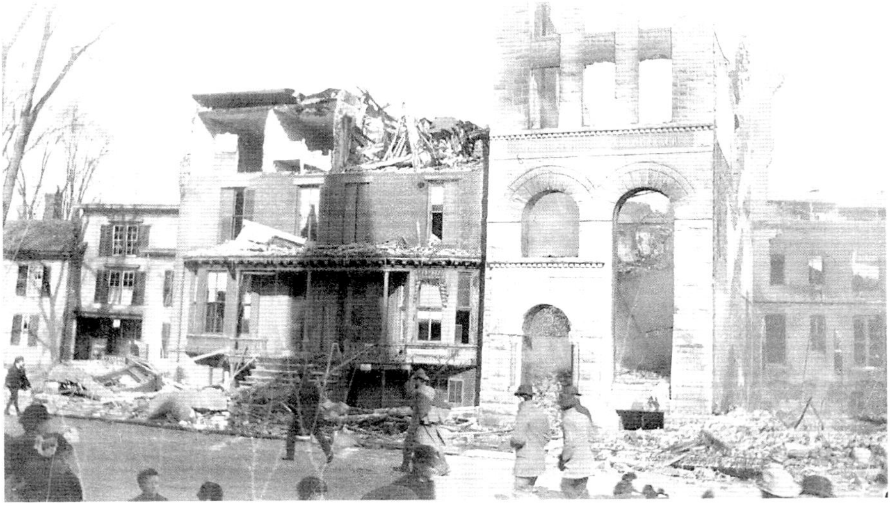

Grand Street, Beyond American Building
West of the American building, the smaller shops were partially burned but unsalvageable. *From the author's collection.*

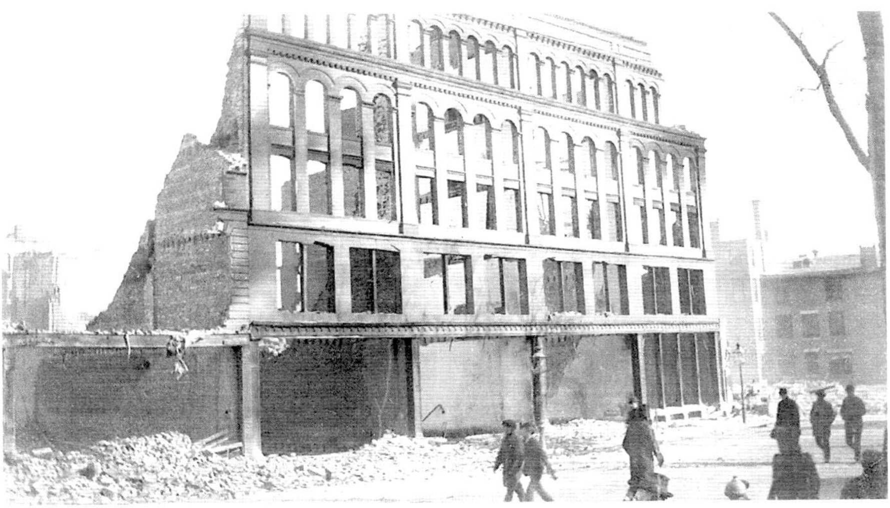

Franklin Building Fire
The Franklin House also suffered heavy losses. *From the author's collection.*

work. The three employees of Reid and Hughes Department Store walked onto Bank Street, eager to end another workday. Within fifteen minutes, the building was afire. Flames shot out from third-floor windows and smoke spewed up from the basement. By the time the first fire truck responded, a full-scale conflagration was in effect.

The wind picked up. Sparks carried the blaze toward the back of the building and quickly ignited the Salvation Army barracks and the local Turkish bath. As more firefighters responded, fire erupted across Bank Street and raced to South Main. According to a news report of the day, the fire engulfed the Ryan and Fitzmaurice block, Cannon and Webster's Drugstore, Davis's Cigar Store and the shop of J.B. Mullings and Sons. The reporter wrote that the fire "jumped across that street, shriveling the buildings like paper."

The fire burned east and west of its origin. When the Masonic Temple caught, the buildings on Grand Street were helpless. Soon that entire block was in ruins. Thirty families stood hopeless as their tenement apartments disappeared in the blaze.

Fire companies responded from throughout the area. Soon the downtown streets were filled with trucks and men from Hartford, New Haven, Bridgeport, Torrington and Naugatuck. At 9:00 p.m. the state's militia was called out to keep order as firefighters discussed blowing up buildings to stop the spread of the flames to the nearby residential neighborhoods and factories.

Partial control was reached by 10:30 p.m., when the flames on South Main were checked. Hope began to form that the fires on Center Street would be the last.

That hope dissipated by midnight. According to the *New York Times* reporter on the scene:

> *Shortly after midnight the fire started in new places, and the efforts of the local firemen, combined with the aid given by fire-fighters and apparatus from the other cities, seemed powerless to stay its progress.*

Panic and rumors quickly spread, citing deaths and injuries that hadn't occurred. Nearby residential neighborhoods watched the sparks from the flames carried along on the wind; each feared it would suffer the same damage that leveled the central business district.

In the end, the fire caused more than $2 million in damages and left the city of forty-five thousand with charred ruins that had, only a day before, been a bustling and prosperous business district.

Chapter Five

ENTERING THE TWENTIETH CENTURY

For fifty years the Industrial Revolution waged, with factories expanding and new citizens settling down to look for work. The city began to grow.

It is easy to imagine that time as "golden." But it was, in truth, a time of extreme contrast. Industrialist families with great wealth inhabited the city's center, and the middle class began to settle up through the Cracker Hill and Overlook sections. Large homes and parks were constructed.

The Overlook section north of downtown bordered the old Cooke Street reservoir. A bold development of homes was constructed at the turn of the century. Queen Anne, Colonial Revival, Tudor Revival and Arts and Crafts houses of ample size, replete with beautiful brass ornamentation, stood smartly along tree-lined streets. Cornelius Cables was the main developer of 148 acres, beginning with a broad avenue separated by a landscaped median. Columbia Boulevard set the standard.

Cables's houses had immediate appeal, more so because the developer secured a trolley line up "Burnt Hill" to the boulevard. Homes were complete with servant quarters, and some houses had eschewed stables in favor of automobile garages. Fulton Park's seventy acres surrounded the old reservoir and were gifted to the city in 1919 by the Fulton family. Frederick Law Olmsted, who designed Central Park and the Columbian Exposition of 1893, created a functional and beautiful respite for the nearby residents.

Farther down the hill, in the Hillside section of town, another Olmsted park was constructed on the Hayden family property after one of the houses burned. Along the hill that rose from downtown to Overlook, mansions abounded, filled with the industrialist families whose factories built fortunes. A constitutional along these streets would bring close contact to the Griggs, Chases, Benedicts, Gosses, Camps, Haydens, Burnhams, Weltons and Scovills. Business leaders and their various relations peppered the hill with distinctive architecture. St. Margaret's School for young ladies provided genteel education.

Chauffeurs drove wives to various clubs and social events. Mansions like Rose Hill loomed on hillsides, looking down over a valley filled with smokestacks spewing clouds of ash. That view meant wealth.

It was also a city filling with tenements that were congested, poorly built and lacking fundamental amenities such as water and adequate sanitary facilities. According to health department records, the children of factory workers often suffered from malnutrition and diseases related to filth. Boils, impetigo, alopecia, diphtheria, tuberculosis and the like were not uncommon.

Child labor was another problem. Brass manufacturing was a hot, dirty, dangerous environment for adults, let alone children. The State of Connecticut passed a law in 1869 that prevented children under the age of fourteen from working in factories unless they had attended school for three months within the previous year. Yet in 1883–84, Scovill reported that its employees included one ten-year-old boy, an eleven-year-old girl and a few thirteen- and fourteen-year-olds in "fetch and carry" positions.

A report from the Waterbury school system acknowledged that many children left school at age fifteen to work. Schooling had been free in Waterbury since 1853, but elementary education wasn't made mandatory until 1868, at a time when schools were seen as the best venue to "Americanize" immigrant children.

Conditions in the nineteenth century meant different things to different people, depending on their economic status in Waterbury. Work was plentiful most of the time, and women made up a good portion of the workforce. But for those in manufacturing, there was a very high risk of injury, the loss of digits or limbs. Workdays were ten hours long with an hour off for lunch. The workweek lasted six days, and the only holidays recognized were Thanksgiving, Christmas, Good Friday and the Fourth of July—all unpaid, of course.

Even after the State of Connecticut decreed workdays not to exceed eight hours without paying overtime, the brass industries demanded more. It was an industry that consistently worked to alleviate the burden of labor costs, sometimes using skilled workers as contractors, making them pay for assistants out of pocket.

To ameliorate their plight, workers formed food co-ops to save money and ensure their security and joined clubs and fraternal orders. Such organizations allowed individuals to take out insurance on their lives and for sickness. By the Gilded Age, nearly 20 percent of the local population supported fifty-four clubs.

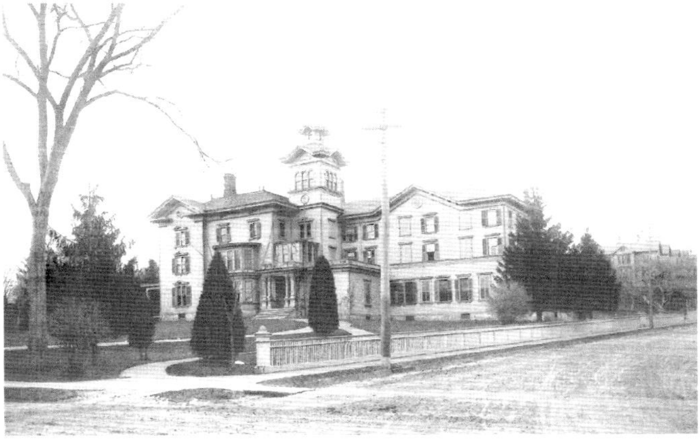

ST. MARGARET'S SCHOOL Fashionable young ladies were taught at the neighborhood academy of St. Margaret's. The school later merged with the McTernan School and moved to Chase Parkway. It is now known as Chase Collegiate. *From* Waterbury and Her Industries.

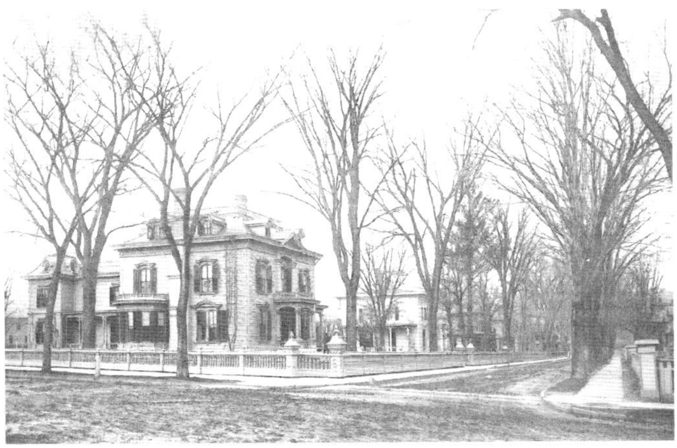

ELTON RESIDENCE The leading citizens erected beautiful mansions from downtown, up through the Hillside neighborhood and into Overlook. This is the Elton home. *From* Waterbury and Her Industries.

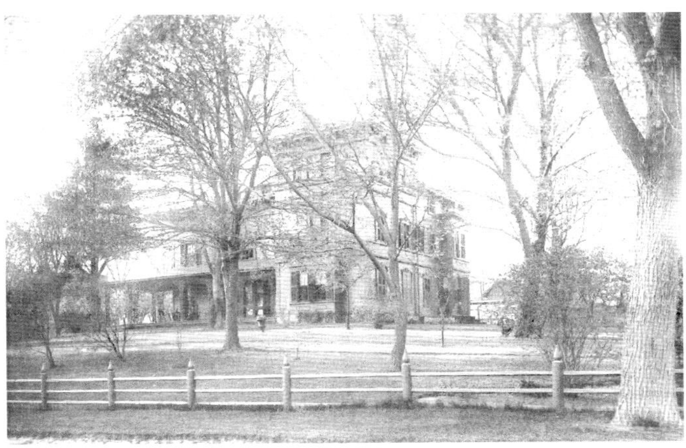

KINGSBURY HOMESTEAD The wealthy in town had enough money to enjoy life. Live-in help performed the daily chores. *From* Waterbury and Her Industries.

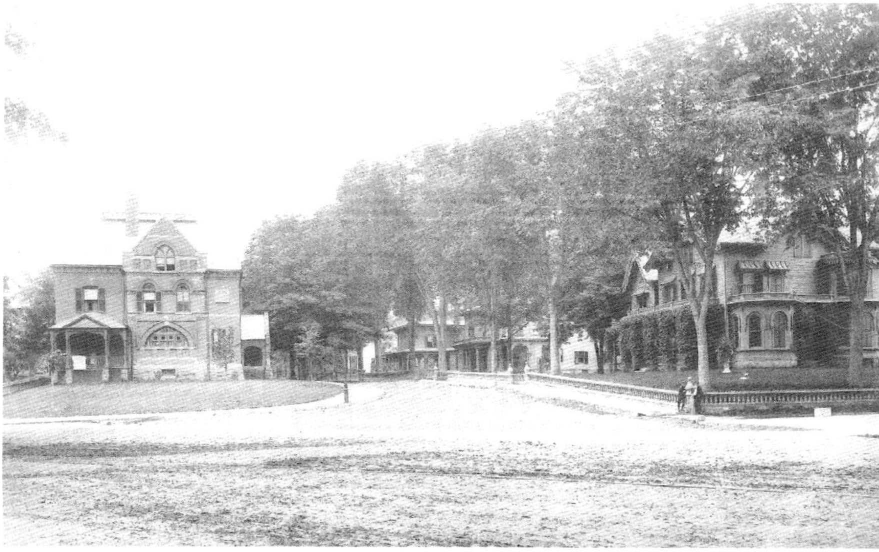

Church Street
This corner faces the green. Just out of sight on the right is St. John's Church with the rectory facing it. This is the street that housed several industrialist families, a short walk from work and shopping. *From* Waterbury and Her Industries.

American workers, whatever their ethnic heritage, had begun to consider forming labor groups for protection. As skilled workers realized their worth to the overall production, the idea formed that industry should pay more. Craft unions had been available for men, specific to a trade. Many workers, however, despite their large numbers within the workforce, were excluded from any consideration. Some of these were the unskilled laborers. Black laborers performed the dirtiest jobs. Others were women. One uniting problem that all workers faced was the threat of mechanization making them obsolete.

In 1882, twenty-four brass spinners held a strike to protest machinery replacing them and decreasing their wages. Four years later, another forty-five workers protested. Both actions were unsuccessful.

One way the Waterbury manufacturers quashed labor unions was by keeping the city an "open shop." This provided the leeway to adjust costs as the market warranted. When a depression affected the economy in 1893, 30 percent of the laborers lost their jobs and the rest lost 25 percent of their wages. Even though one thousand people filled the green to demonstrate against the move, nothing changed.

In 1903, another technological change caused turmoil.

Horse-drawn trolleys were first welcomed in the community because they offered greater mobility to everyone. The wealthy could move out of town to more rural settings, away from the smoke and smells that made up their income. The poor could travel greater distances to find work. But when railroad workers (of which trolley operators qualified) went on strike, public sentiment turned ugly. Their opinion was voiced violently when a mob attacked a downtown trolley, stoning it with bricks until a militia broke up the riot.

As factories grew, so did the cities. Waterbury's geological footprint defined the city. The river plain initially housed everything until the space was taken over by business and manufacturing.

Utilizing space was very important in Waterbury as the population continued to swell from five thousand in 1850 to twenty thousand following World War I. Middle-class homeowners made the most of each parcel, constructing triple-deckers to house three families at a time. This allowed the rental property to augment the owner's income, thus allowing working families a way to build a nest egg.

The steady swell of immigrant workers flooding to the city was housed in congested tenements that brought a host of problems to the cities, straining the services to the utmost.

It was time for the city to take on the mantle of civic responsibility. Firefighting had been voluntary, with small companies of men forming "clubs" that often used fires as a competition of speed and skill. Manufacturers as large as Scovill relied on their own fire companies.

Health was the overriding issue. Disease affected the workforce and stood in the way of production. A lack of sanitary systems and delivery of pure water drove health risks high. The city began building its infrastructure immediately following the Civil War. A municipal water system was constructed in 1868 using East Mountain Reservoir and Cooke Street Pond as reservoirs.

Though he wasn't the first, Robert Cairns was considered the father of Waterbury's water system. From 1890 to 1937, Cairns served the city. When calculating the productivity of the two existing reservoirs, he determined them inadequate for a population of over thirty thousand. His answer to this dilemma was bold.

Cairns drew up a plan to bring water from the Shepaug River beneath Bantam Lake, through Morris and into Waterbury. This system was accomplished by blasting tunnels large enough to hold trains underground from the river into Waterbury, where the water is dispersed through an underground pipe system. The achievement inspired accolades from

Cairns's colleagues across the globe, and by the time his tenure with the city was through, the water system provided enough for the 100,000 citizens the town would eventually hold.

Water wasn't Cairns's only concern. Sewage had also become a serious problem. Most dwellings relied on cesspools, but by 1893 twenty-six miles of sewage pipe were laid and connected to over two thousand homes. Cairns's design increased the underground network of collecting waste and sending it into the Naugatuck River, after which a suit brought by the Platt family forced the city to construct a waste treatment center. Cairns's design was utilitarian in nature. He reasoned that with all the industries of the Naugatuck Valley pumping chemicals and poisons into the river, the waste was the least of the problems. The treatment plant only had to break waste down enough not to clog the mill wheels.

In the 1880s, amenities such as parks were added to the town. The green served for centuries as the first and only public park in the city. Recreational parks were constructed, funded by horse trolley companies, and provided reasons for people to use the transportation system on their days off.

Later, through bequests, Hamilton Park, Chase Park, Fulton Park and Library Park were donated for public use.

The railroad company in town constructed a new Union Station, designed by the notable architectural firm McKim, Meade and White. The distinctive building along the track contains a unique bell tower modeled after one in Sienna, Italy.

The building of a new train station launched a wave of public construction and city beautification. Henry Sabin Chase saw the opportunity to create a magnificent gateway into the city. Cairns worked closely with the industrialist, first widening the avenue leading from the train into the heart of downtown and christening it Grand Street. Older small buildings and those destroyed in the 1902 fire were replaced with larger, more substantial constructions. Chase had admired the architectural work of architect Cass Gilbert and selected him as the designer.

Gilbert's designs and vision were in keeping with the City Beautiful style set forth at the Columbian Exposition (Chicago World's Fair) in 1893. This fair commemorated the 400th anniversary of Columbus's discovery of the New World, and the United States was proudly showing its technological lead in the world, as well as a main concourse filled with structures of classical, Beaux Arts style called the White City. The fair set the tone of architectural styles, city planning and amusement parks for decades to come.

After arsonist Bernard Murray burned down the city hall, Chase saw an opportunity to include the replacement in the "Grand" plan. The overall plan was sweeping in scope. After disembarking from the train, a visitor would be greeted by a spacious avenue leading into the city. The curved façade of the American Brass Building on the north side of the street drew the eye forward. A small stone gazebo provided entrance to the newly formed Library Park surrounding the Bronson mansion that now served as a public library. Beyond the Bronson Library stood the Cass Gilbert city hall, a handsome brick and limestone creation fronted by a fountain and appointed with classic lines and a cupola on top. The Chase Brass headquarters stood directly opposite city hall, on the north side. A manicured lawn protected by a wrought-iron fence surrounded the large office building. Chase deliberately urged Gilbert to create a design that was simpler in style so as not to compete with the handsome new city building.

Gilbert went on to build a bank and two smaller brick buildings (Lincoln House and the Chase Dispensary) along the side of city hall. The post office sat beyond the bank, and across from this a bank retail space sported myriad styles that were in keeping with the overall grand design. Visitors to the city could not help but be impressed.

The work didn't stop. A few decades later, the old post office was replaced by a magnificent Art Deco design.

A swelling population with plenty of work attracted diversions, such as traveling shows and activities. Theatrical performances abounded in every neighborhood and organizations provided diversions that included sports as well as the arts.

It was a time of invention. The first telephone was installed in town in 1877, and electric lights replaced gas lamps on streets in 1884.

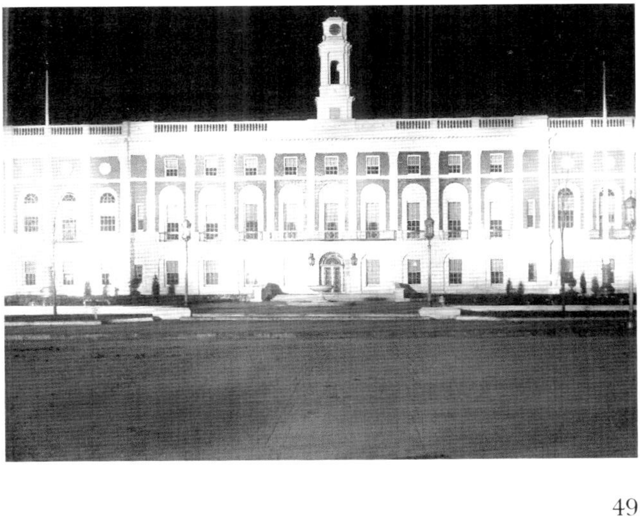

CITY HALL
This is the earliest photo of the completed city hall. Cass Gilbert created a lasting masterpiece in the City Beautiful style, which Henry Sabin Chase so admired that he would not allow his executive offices across the street to compete with its opulence. *From the author's collection.*

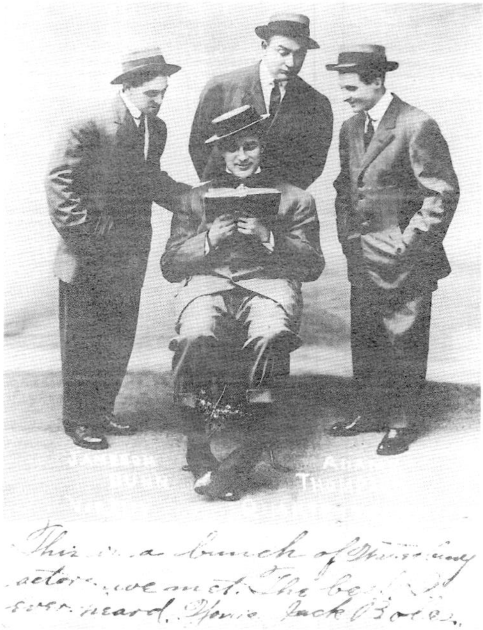

Actors
Local entertainments attracted people from throughout the region to Waterbury's theaters. *From the author's collection.*

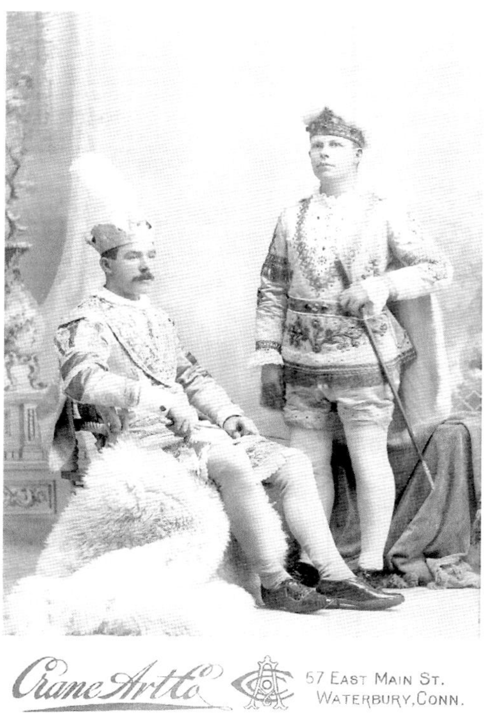

Actors
Workers braced with wages could visit a variety of burlesque-type entertainment. The fun found in town gave Waterbury the title "Sin City." *From the author's collection.*

But everyone was not on an upward path. Orphans and families in need were often overlooked. Churches urged the wealthy to succor the weak and frail. Organizations began to form that allowed people to help themselves. Following the end of the Civil War, the Waterbury Industrial School opened to hone the employment skills of young women. The Boys Club provided shelter for homeless boys starting in 1889. Hospital care in Waterbury began in earnest in 1890, when Waterbury Hospital opened its doors, followed by St. Mary's Hospital in 1909.

Health concerns were very real. In 1917, a most unexpected epidemic put the greatest strain on Waterbury and nearly every other city in the world. It was hoped that improved public sanitation and available healthcare would provide a measure of safety, but during the months of September 1918 through May of the following year, Waterbury was not immune to the influenza pandemic that swept the world. People today recognize this pandemic by the name Spanish flu, a title bestowed when the disease spread from France to Spain, and media reports touted the vast number of deaths. Until this stage, the illness was ignored so as not to detract from the world war being waged.

The Spanish flu killed more people than either the Black Plague or World War I. The number of people contracting the disease reached beyond fifty million souls, and in some remote areas, entire villages were wiped out. The loss of life represented 5 percent of the human population.

The lack of media coverage, coupled with soldiers shipping off to war, helped spread the disease globally. It was a swift-moving illness that would run its course in an area within a month, sometimes killing victims within a day of manifesting symptoms.

Unlike other flu illnesses that adversely affect the very young and old, this one felled the young and strong, attacking their immune systems. Class lines were breached; both the poor and nobility died. Those who survived the initial flu sometimes fell during the ensuing pneumonia caused by a compromised immune system. This particular strain caused mucous membranes to bleed, and victims bled from the ears, nose, stomach and intestines.

Approximately 115,720 people contracted the disease in Connecticut, and it is estimated that as many as 11,000 died. Over 5,000 succumbed in October 1918 alone. Waterbury was particularly hard hit.

The effect on a community during that time was unprecedented. Hospitals were short staffed as workers contracted the disease, yet wards filled quickly with the sick and dying. Cemeteries were hard pressed to find ample numbers of coffins and to bury the bodies.

The annual health reports submitted to Mayor William A.H. Sandland from Health Director C.W.S. Frost are low-keyed but grim. The previous reports make no mention of influenza as a cause of death, but in 1918 Frost's description begins with accounting for 10 percent of the deaths of infants as caused by influenza and pneumonia.

In town, the number of cases totaled 6,182 for influenza, with 775 deaths resulting. Pneumonia, which often followed the bout of flu, claimed 673 victims, with 236 dying. By contrast, the next leading cause of death from illness came from diphtheria—192 people caught it, and 15 died.

Trying to explain the phenomenon to the mayor, the report read:

> *During the month of September, 1918 there commenced an epidemic of Influenza that gradually gathering force swept over this City so that scarcely a single family escaped having at least one case, and in a large number of instances every member of the family developed the disease. A large number of cases were complicated with the "Captain of the Men of Death" pneumonia and in a very malignant form, so that the toll of deaths exacted was enormous.*
>
> *The first cases were reported on September 25th and from then on up to November 1st there were 6,182 cases of Influenza reported and 6732 cases of Pneumonia with a report of 95 deaths. The epidemic still continues and the full history can only be given in a later report.*

To alleviate the strain on the community's health services, an isolation hospital opened, and twenty-one patients were admitted, immediately followed by more patients on a steady basis until the ninety-four beds were filled within the first twenty-four hours of operation. The Chase Park Hospital, as it was called, was equipped with a nursing and kitchen staff, at first supplied by Red Cross nurses and volunteers who were quickly supplanted by the Triangle Force from Scovill Manufacturing Co.

The numbers show how desperate the situation was. In October, 220 patients were placed in isolation, 75 died, 33 went on to convalescent care and 120 were discharged.

Some of those patients were discharged to the Country Club after members voted to open the facility for convalescent care during the course of the epidemic.

Frost remarked that in the hospital's first day of operation, thirty-six patients succumbed, "showing the severity of the cases admitted and the haste with which they were rushed to the hospital."

It wasn't until the very end of World War I that workers began to grumble all over the country and serious turmoil developed. Waterbury's initial

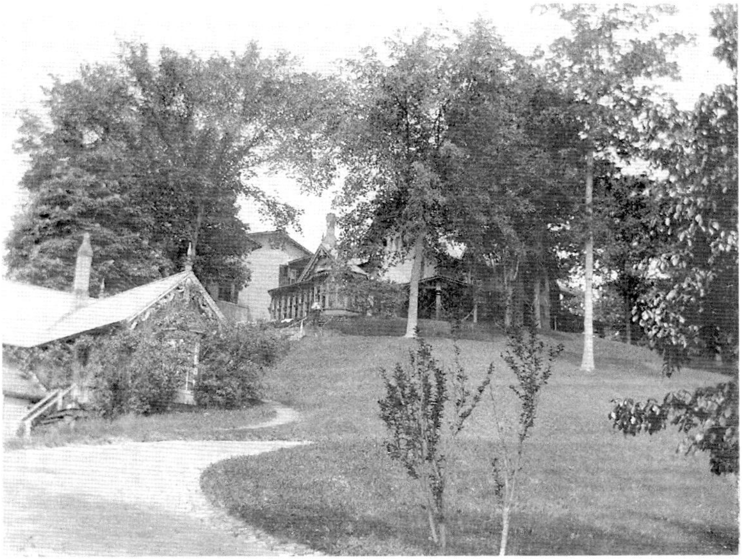

Waterbury Hospital Entrance
The entrance to the hospital was more residential, a far cry from today's utilitarian complex. *From the author's collection.*

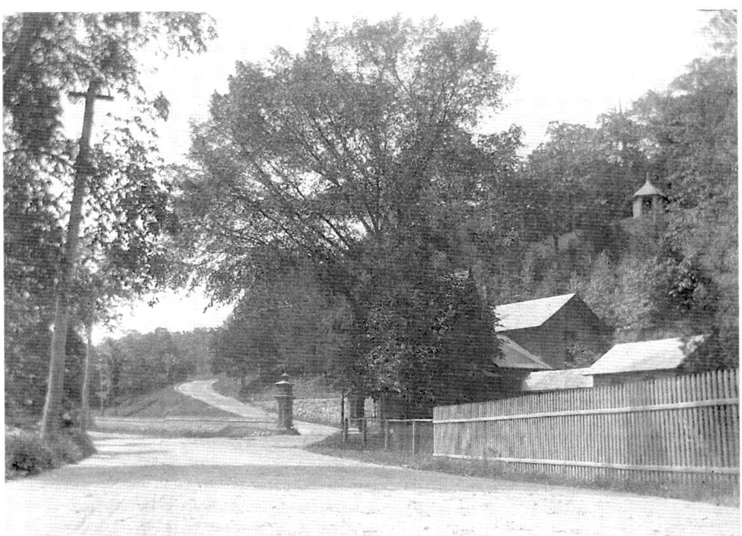

Waterbury Hospital
When Waterbury Hospital was built at the end of the nineteenth century, the setting was more a bucolic retreat. The original structure was a luxurious estate. *From the author's collection.*

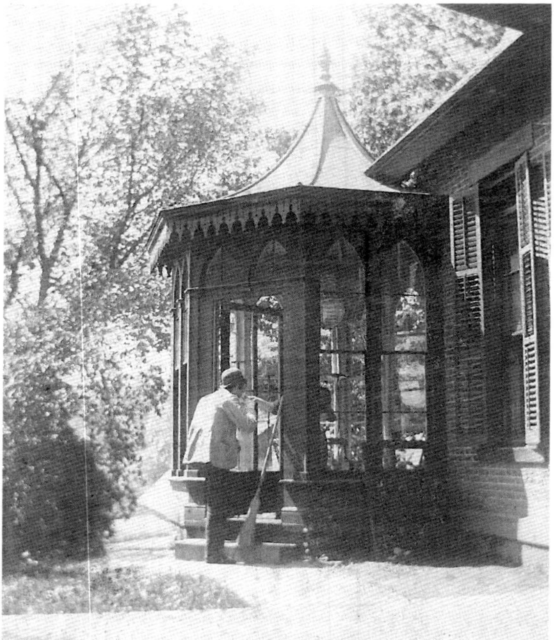

Left: WATERBURY HOSPITAL
It is hard to imagine this setting as one equipped for trauma. *From the author's collection.*

Below: REAR OF WATERBURY HOSPITAL
The backside of the original hospital shows the patients' wing. *From the author's collection.*

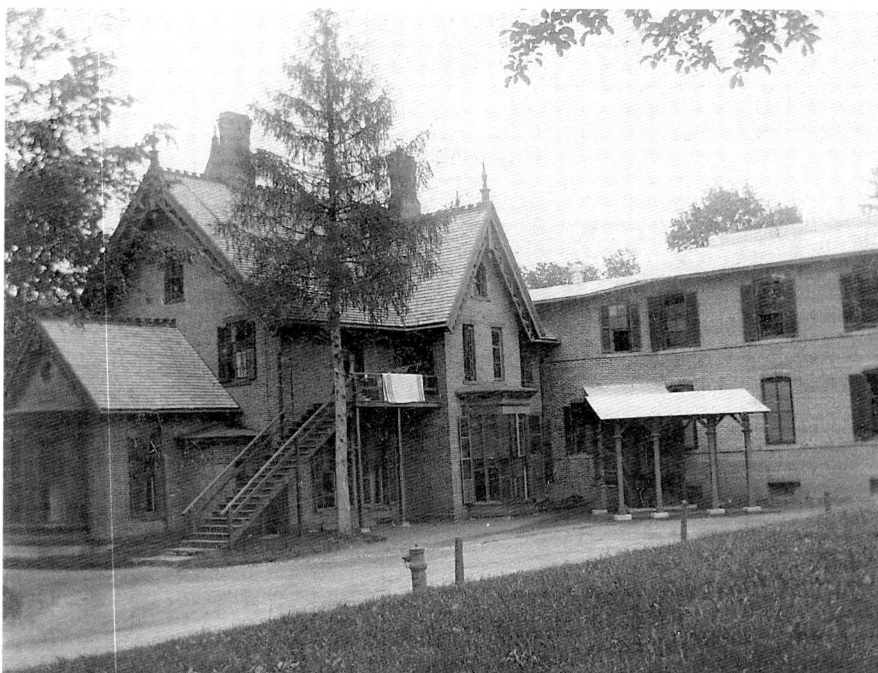

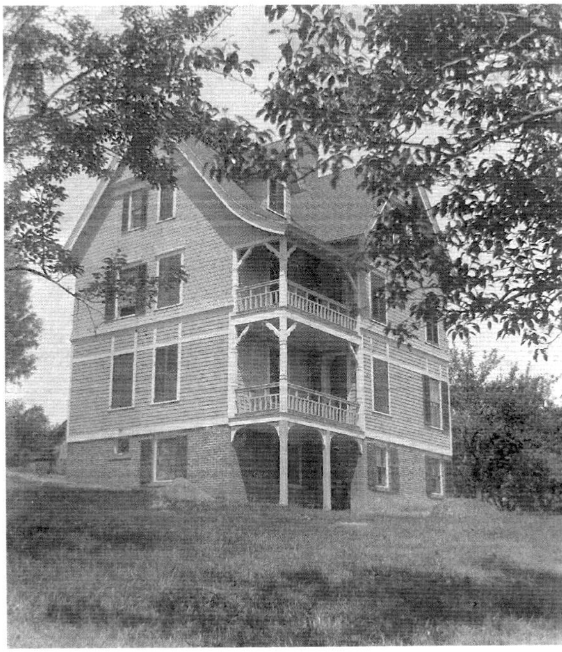

Right: NURSES' HOME
The Nurses' Home allowed staff to be close by. *From the author's collection.*

Below: HOSPITAL LAUNDRY
Even the original bar was employed as the laundry. *From the author's collection.*

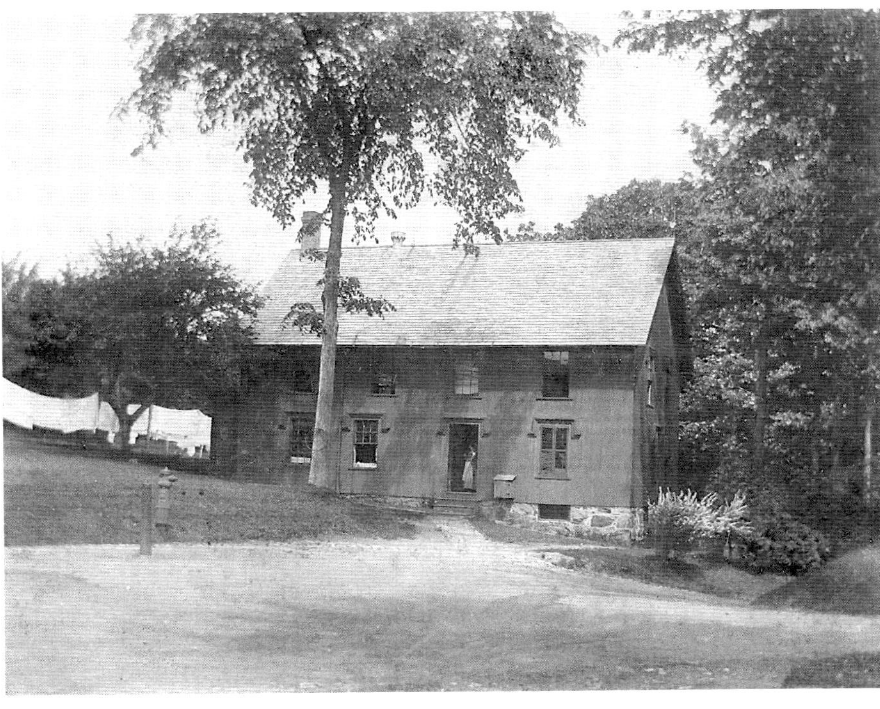

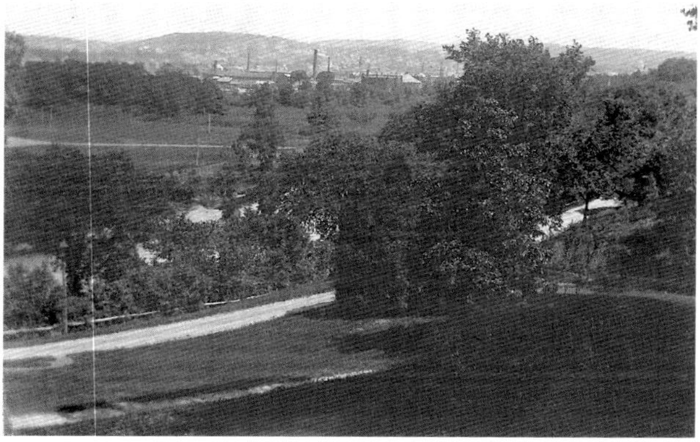

View of Waterbury
This is the original view from Waterbury Hospital. Despite its rural location, patients and staff could look over the city that spawned their existence. *From the author's collection.*

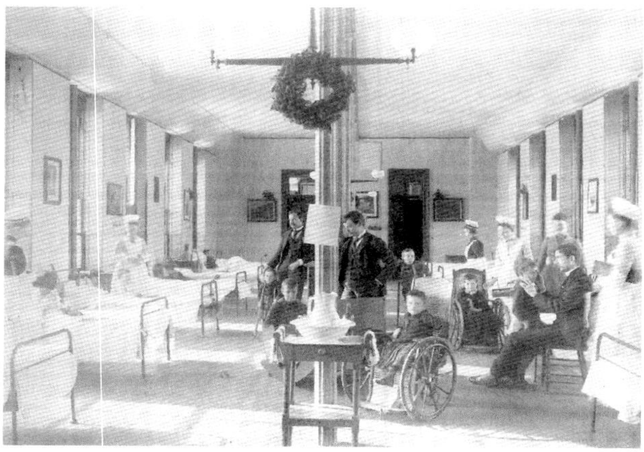

Pediatric Ward
The pediatric ward at Christmas demonstrates the homey touch in what, at that time, was a modern medical ward. *From the author's collection.*

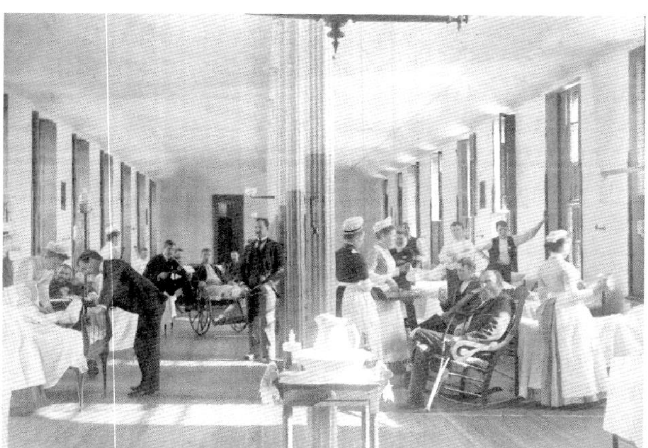

Orthopedic Ward
The orthopedic ward at Waterbury Hospital displays the spacious interior. Patients' wards were similar in design, allowing for good ventilation if not for privacy. *From the author's collection.*

response was to raise wages, and this caused the health inspector, Dr. Frost, to remark that this act resulted in fewer cases of malnutrition.

But it was a long way to what one might deem a "healthful" lifestyle. Dr. Frost cited the poorly ventilated, filthy living conditions as contributing to the illnesses in children. To counteract poor health within the schools, an Open Air program was launched at Clark School for fifty students suffering from the worst neglect. Participants were taught in a ventilated classroom and fed breakfast every morning. The children were encouraged to drink milk throughout the day and to rest periodically. Each child was bathed weekly and monitored for disease. Those with tuberculosis were sent to sanitariums.

As each child progressed, he or she was returned to the regular classrooms and a child on the waiting list filled the available Open Air seat.

It was not a humanitarian gesture entirely. A good part of the reasoning for this program and the need to improve the lives of children was smart business sense. Healthy children meant a stronger workforce for the local factories. They were also less taxing on the community's services.

Health reports to Mayor Sandland in 1918 cited a need for more money to be spent per capita on health. Waterbury had been spending a "ridiculously small" twelve and a half cents per person, an amount adequate for a population of five thousand. Waterbury required seventy-five cents. A small increase was granted, and the new budget provided fifteen cents per person. Compared to Bridgeport's allocation of fifty cents for its citizens, Waterbury's raise seemed begrudging.

Dr. Frost had grave concerns regarding the health of the city's inhabitants, writing, "The rapid increase in industrial progress has been accompanied by the many problems and dangers that complicated health conditions of the mixed population of the modern manufacturing cities."

Life was hard for laborers during the first part of this century. Business was booming and cities were growing. Municipal governments were striving to improve the infrastructures such as sanitation, water and gas lines. But for the poor, these changes were remote and sometimes out of reach.

The average family was hard pressed. Husbands had work, especially during World War I when the brass manufacturers provided shell casings for arms. Wives had a full array of chores. It was a city of stark contrast. On one side there was a multitude of mansions and brick factories. On the other, the townspeople lived on what could be called urban farms. Even today one can find the remnants of barns in backyards that, when they were constructed, housed horses for transportation, cows for milk, chickens for eggs and swine for meat. And in every barn was a set of stalls that needed to be shoveled. A woman living during this period had little time for leisure. She had a home to maintain and meals to prepare. Her pantry did not contain ready-made meals in a box. A chicken dinner meant killing the chicken, plucking it and cooking it over a hot oven. Grocery shopping was a task performed locally, often on a daily basis with the woman hand-carrying home bags of goods, crossing muddy streets peppered with horse droppings. Older children were impressed into service at home, performing menial chores and babysitting. Women's lives were quite different from the routines of "soccer moms" today who organize their children's playtime in a regimental fashion. One early newspaper report in 1907 illustrates this difference.

On a cold Sunday morning in October, a group of children played behind the icehouse on Seery Street, near the train terminal. The icehouse property ended in a steep embankment along the Mahan Canal. The canal was ten feet deep and swift moving. A shout from the children caught the attention of the local policeman on duty. Officer Cavanaugh saw a child thrashing in the water, five hundred feet away. It was a toddler, and the child's two young companions were frantic. Cavanaugh dove into the canal and rescued the child, returning young Frank Laborda Jr. to his mother. The toddler was sixteen months old and had been in the care of siblings, who themselves were not yet beyond grade school.

Garbage collection was done by the city's nine horse-drawn wagons and, in winter, by one of three sleighs. Private contractors helped for free, claiming the garbage they collected to feed their swine. The health department worked at maintaining sanitary conditions, inspecting food and vendors. Today's violations seem petty given the nature of some early citations, such as one warning milk vendors in contact with smallpox to wash their hands.

Blight and unsanitary conditions posed great concern for the city, as did venereal disease. Waterbury joined forces in 1919 with both the federal and state governments to help stop the spread of sexually transmitted diseases.

That same year, following the dire numbers of cases of Spanish flu, the health director reported that the number of flu cases dropped to 941 and pneumonia cases numbered 108. A total of 58 Waterburians died in 1918, a dramatic decrease from the year before that marked a return to normal and a chance to plan for the future.

Planning for the future was a constant struggle for those in Waterbury. With so many dependent on the industrial base for a livelihood, it was incumbent on the factory owners to keep finding ways to make money. Wartime profits would only last so long, and the swell of workers placing a strain on the city's resources made it essential to continually develop new products.

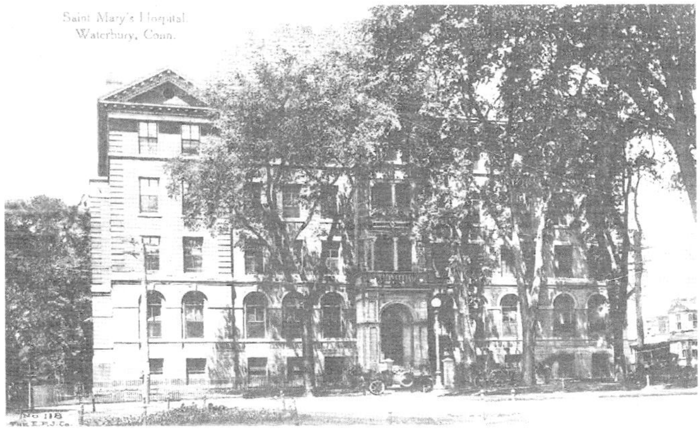

OLD ST. MARY'S HOSPITAL
St. Mary's Hospital provided a "Catholic" hospital for local workers and their families. *From the author's collection.*

Chase Brass stands out in modern times as an innovator. It was a Johnny-come-lately manufacturing concern that started when Augustus Sabin Chase and investors acquired the local U.S. Button Company. Augustus's son, Henry Sabin Chase, who worked with Cairns to forge a grand visage for the city, supplanted his tenure as president.

When his leadership began in 1896, the company was renamed the Waterbury Manufacturing Company and the button line was expanded to include rolling brass. Until the twentieth century, the company stood out from the others by the giant Percheron horses that pulled the Chase wagons.

At the end of World War I, the United States government remained the company's largest customer, but diversification was necessary. The retooling began in 1928 with the introduction of the new company logo, a centaur launching an arrow skyward. In 1929, with little progress made to a peacetime production line, the company was sold to Kennecott Copper and renamed Chase Brass and Copper. Frederick Chase managed the company locally.

Chase began producing components for the auto industry. A subsequent line of production proved long lasting and built on the technology of chrome plating. Chase developed Art Deco–styled housewares fashioned by the leading designers of the day.

Chase's wares design was European in origin but was quickly adopted by Americans because it represented a sleek, functional style of the future. The metalware had a copper base coated with chromium and adorned at times with Bakelite, making the product extremely durable and long lasting, as well as useful for serving hot foods and drink. It was an inexpensive alternative to silver, shiny without polishing and useful. The product line was booming by 1936, and its popularity as a collectable endures to the present day.

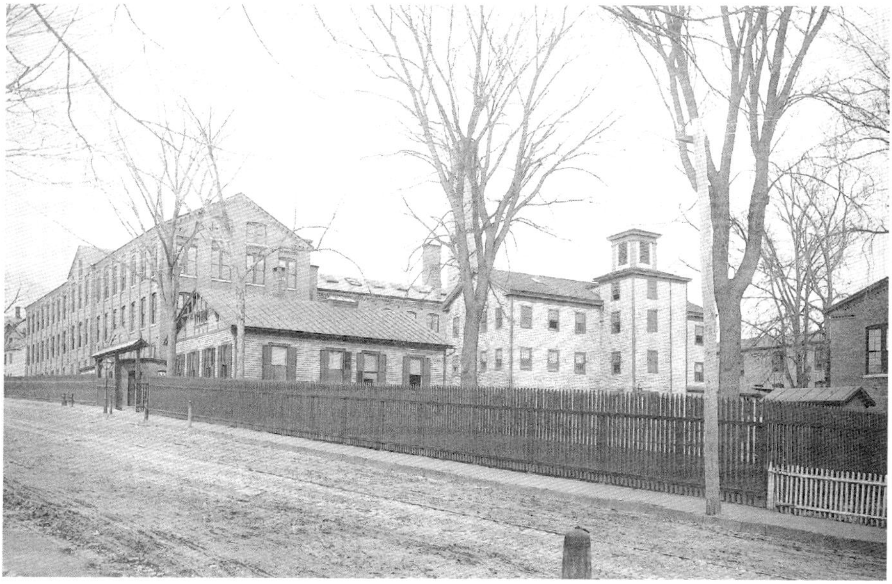

Waterbury Manufacturing
In 1896, the Chase family assumed control of Waterbury Manufacturing. *From* Waterbury and Her Industries.

At Scovill, two men forged a partnership that was reminiscent of the founding days of the company. They set the stage for the company's expansion into the next century. Chauncey Porter Goss and Mark Leavenworth Sperry, like the Scovill brothers before them, had personality differences that complemented each other and that were beneficial to the company. One was content at home, in Waterbury, administering to the company, while the other was more urbane and a true promoter. Starting as clerks and later running the company until 1918, the pair, according to the company's history, "achieved great strides, growing and expanding during the last quarter of the 19th century and gaining great financial gains during the first decades of the 20th century."

They invested in mechanization and improvements and diversified into areas of aluminum sheeting, electrically conductive wire and lamp burners. The World War I boon allowed the company to compete with larger brass industries, and by the war's end Scovill's revenue had grown to eight times what it had been before the war.

The stage was set for Waterbury to move into a modern age.

Chapter Six

LABOR UNREST AND POSTWAR BUSINESS

The rise in population during the nineteenth century and into the twentieth century was due to an influx of immigrants needed for the workforce. The first wave brought the Irish escaping the Great Famine.

Initially unwelcome, they took work digging canals and laying track for the railroad. Some made their way into industry, such as Daniel Bergan, who lived with and worked for the Platts in their mill. The Italians, Lithuanians, French Canadians, Germans and Russians followed the Irish, all looking to make their fortunes but bringing with them their own cultural identities. Even poor African Americans made their way north in the wake of the Civil War.

By 1850, one-quarter of the Waterbury population was foreign born. By 1890, 70 percent of the population was made up of immigrants or first-generation Americans. Americanizing the workforce was the next step.

New workers arriving in Waterbury were initially housed in crowded, dark tenements. Work hours were long, tiring and dirty. Church and social clubs provided entertainment of a modest sort, but Waterbury was also filled with saloons and other boisterous entertainments.

Once married, the job of the factory worker was to bolster his family's security and build wealth. With the Catholicism the predominant religion among the immigrants, large families were encouraged. But for the labor class, the small steps in advancing one's economic condition in Waterbury were slowly gained. The proximity to the very wealthy class in town could only aggravate the workers when compared to the humble living conditions of the poor.

For laborers spending ten hours in intense heat under the filthiest conditions, returning home to poverty rankled. Being forced to work long days with no extra pay meant hardship for the entire family, and when industrialists failed to make improvements in the conditions, grumbling began in earnest.

World War I was the galvanizing event.

Most of the workers in Waterbury came from and had family living in European countries with strict, despotic governments. The overthrow of these governments, as in Russia and Italy, offered hope that the working class would see a fairer distribution of wealth.

Much to the consternation of the socialists and fascists, America remained neutral throughout most of the war but contributed to the fighting effort by selling arms to the Allies. Waterbury, in particular, prospered from the war.

Labor agitators wooed disgruntled workers, and American laborers were encouraged to make a political stand through sabotage. In one case, lumberjacks spiked spruce trees to make them unusable for building military airplanes. With so much of the local economy dependent on military contracts, Waterbury industrialists took a grim view of such actions.

Disenfranchised workers who were shut out from trade unions and flirted with socialism could turn to a newly formed, more political union called the International Workers of the World (IWW, or the Wobblies as they were known). This union sought out workers throughout America, especially those working at the lowest levels. Demonstrations and wildcat strikes were encouraged.

Sabotage happened locally on June 2, 1920, at the Hillside Avenue home of John H. Goss, the general manager of Scovill, when a partial stick of dynamite with a battery and wire was detonated outside the sun porch of his large brick home. Goss was in at the time with his wife and children, plus some their school friends from Westover.

The police responded immediately and prepared for future anarchist attacks in town by building an arsenal of five machine guns, 160 riot rifles and forty extra men. Given the size of the bomb against the formidable structure of the house, the detonation served as a threat. Elsewhere in the country, the threats turned into a class war.

It was unclear whether the bomb was an act of union terrorism or a personal statement against the Scovill boss. John H. Goss and his brother Edward had entered Scovill and had ridden to its highest levels. The Scovill family continued to have a family member as a director, but it was the descendants of Chauncey Porter Goss who took the company's helm. The Goss family became the majority stockholders, outnumbering the Scovill seats. Edward O. Goss and his brother John H. were well suited to the task of leading the company into the modern age. John H. had started work as an apprentice in the tool machine shop before ascending to the level of assistant supervisor in 1903. His specialty was efficiency through science.

By 1908, Goss had ascertained that the day-to-day running of Scovill was inefficient and therefore costly. The factory yards were filled with people roaming about looking to catch the eye of a foreman and gain a day's work or family members toting lunch to hungry workers. Foremen often favored members of their ethnic group or hired friends or relatives needing work. If someone didn't have connections, a bribe would grease the wheels.

The first move toward efficiency was setting up an office for a general superintendent, a move that separated management from the day-to-day operations of the plant. In 1909, Goss was named to this position, with his keen support of scientific methods overcoming his lack of an engineering degree.

Changes were made. A casting plant was rebuilt. Furnaces were switched to more efficient methods, finally resulting in a continuous casting system. Research began on new firing processes. And artisans who used traditional methods were replaced, elevating non-skilled workers into the semiskilled level, which employed techniques that were more repetitive and scientific.

When those changes resulted in efficient production and higher profits, Goss made another bold move. He moved his office to the heart of the plant and had foremen report directly to him. He formed a foremen's association in 1913 that offered the men their own restaurant/clubhouse, complete with billiards and other games. As the men were lulled into a sense of camaraderie with the general supervisor, Goss stripped them of their great power on the plant floor.

The factory foremen had been in charge of hiring, production schedules and quality control. By inserting another layer of management to oversee the time-keeping duties, hiring and work progress, the foremen would be reduced to a level without perks. What they gained was more responsibility over indirect labor costs.

The new move toward more efficient operations included the hiring of more women. Goss's logic was to make the timekeepers distinct from the workmen. Women clerical workers would be housed on the factory floor but segregated from the men. They would dress in business attire, visibly making them distinct from the blue-collar workers.

Chronometers and scientific research began to record how long it took to perform rote tasks, and pressure was brought to bear on the workers to perform to maximum capacity. They were to report to work and record their hours accurately using time clocks.

Women segued into managerial positions within this department, such as Helen Duncan, who oversaw the welfare of women by forming a Girls' Club for bowling and basketball. Later, women oversaw workers' housing and other amenities.

For Goss, the watchwords were control and efficiency. By 1919, Scovill had installed a communication system of nine hundred telephones, with two switchboards and four operators. Employee numbers were assigned to individuals, and through this they were tracked for payroll, employment history and statistical data.

Professional development was important, especially since newer scientific equipment was constantly being introduced to make the processes more accurate and streamlined. With many of these tasks performed by women, promoting from within allowed female plant workers to attain office jobs by way of testing.

Goss inserted a new clerical layer to the factory whose cost was borne by the money saved from factory workers. While it provided clean, safe employment for some, it placed a burden on those whose labor provided the pay.

The attack on Goss followed the arrest of 140 men the previous month when police arrested strike agitators. At the time, nearly a quarter of the workforce was on strike as manufacturers entered a postwar lull that coincided with inflation and work cutbacks. At Scovill, the unskilled workers demanded a pay raise from forty-five cents per hour to seventy-five cents.

The workers' strike in the Naugatuck Valley began in Ansonia Copper and Brass but spread to include thousands in Waterbury. The strike lasted weeks, and as money ran out, workers would return to the job a day or two at a time. In context with the rest of the country, Waterbury's strike was minimal. Elsewhere, anarchy prompted industry strikes that were joined by sympathetic workers who shut down city services.

This was the beginning of the labor movement in Waterbury, a movement that would not reach its full strength until the late 1940s and early '50s.

In the pre-Depression days there was an ebb and flow of national economics and local labor relations. The great money earned during war production was needed for retooling to peacetime production. Company owners believed that the earnings of workers during the heady days needed to be decreased following the law of supply and demand. Workers believed that the profits gleaned from the war should be spent on better pay and job security.

Coinciding with the economic changes following the First World War came scientific improvements, whereby machinery replaced men, especially in the unskilled areas. Workers were challenged to reach a semiskilled level, and those performing the dirtiest, most backbreaking tasks in the brass industry found themselves out of jobs or with pay cuts that impoverished them.

Before laws were passed that enforced the workers' rights to organize and bargain for higher wages and benefits, company owners were able to appeal to cities for help squashing labor unrest. Waterbury employed the local police force to keep out union agitators and to threaten dissident employees. It was seen as a civic responsibility. The taxes large companies paid into the general fund and the power these companies wielded kept the cities growing and running.

But the unrest was there. And there were several factors at play.

The initial wave of immigrants coming over from Europe to resettle and work in America had been replaced by an influx of black farm workers moving north to escape the economic hard times in the South and to avoid the increased number of lynchings taking place.

This wave of new people had a way of unsettling not only fellow workers but also neighborhoods in general. Waterbury had always been and remains a city filled with distinctive neighborhoods that had taken on the "feel" of the particular people inhabiting them.

Town Plot, which had once been a Yankee stronghold, had changed its ethnic makeup to Italian. Mill Plain Yankees gave way to Irish workers. Long Hill had changed from Italian to black, as did the North End.

And there were neighborhoods that operated with a multiethnic population, such as Overlook, where first the Irish and Jewish resided and then, in modern times, many Puerto Ricans moved in.

The crowding of the city also contributed to some unrest. The population had grown to over 28,000 people when the twentieth century arrived. By the close of World War I, those numbers had risen to over 90,000, passing the 100,000 mark by 1950.

Another source of employee agitation was the management plan to keep workers in a disorganized state. Large companies saw the value of creating "class" distinctions between skilled and unskilled workers, between ethnic groups and between women and men. The large corporations also broke up the factories into smaller, specialized shops that discouraged general organization.

Not all tactics were negative. Scovill provided employees with a plant hospital and created a "foreman's association" to provide recreations. Other companies followed suit, and soon the factories had their own bands, newspapers, libraries and classes in English, as well as housing for families and single men. Scovill row houses still stand on Wood and Ivy Streets and were sold for $4,500; single men were housed in barracks and were charged fifty cents a week for lodging and a shower. Later, YMCA hotel rooms were employed.

Scovill also implemented "the right to challenge" for workers who felt that midlevel management decisions might be denigrating or unfair.

Overall, management operated under a policy of "rationalization." It saw the twentieth century as a time when machinery would replace workers, unskilled workers would gain more expertise and skilled workers would not be so specialized. Science was encouraged over guesswork and tradition. Advance planning and modernization were key. Horses were replaced by trucks; wood furnaces were replaced by oil. And time studies made production more efficient.

Time magazine reported that shrewd Yankee management kept Scovill profitable. Though not duplicating its wartime peak of $13 million in profit, when the Great Depression hit it still showed $1 million in the black.

The local decisions were made against a backdrop of a larger national shift in labor relations. As fascism and socialism in Europe grew in power and popularity, and old monarchies and ways were changed in favor of workers' rights, the American workers recognized their value in making this country grow and wanted to justly share in the rewards.

Political factions clamored to address workers, and speaking engagements in major cities were planned. To get the message across that the unions were unafraid of those in leadership, terror tactics were employed, such as detonating bombs at private homes prior to the rallies.

To stem this tide of anarchy, the government developed the Espionage and Sedition Acts. A new attorney general was named, a man known as a liberal-thinking friend of the workingman. A. Mitchell Palmer of Pennsylvania came into the job just as thirty-eight bombs exploded after being sent through the U.S. postal system. One explosion occurred outside his own home, killing the bomber and making Palmer acutely aware of the recklessness of the agitators.

Working closely with a young attorney, J. Edgar Hoover, Palmer launched a series of raids beginning on November 7, 1919, the second anniversary of the Russian Revolution. Waterbury was one of the cities targeted by Palmer, and with the help of local police, six local workers were apprehended for little more than agitating dissention among immigrant laborers. After heated interrogations and a trial, Palmer sent many of the immigrant dissidents out of the country on what was called the Soviet Ark, a steamship named the *Buford* that was commissioned to take its passengers as close to Russia as possible to let them find their way to a Red Paradise.

When the war ended and conditions for workers remained the same, socialists in America were disillusioned with capitalism.

The contraction of the economy after the expansion during wartime years left millions out of work and impoverished. Inflation set in, and when wages didn't meet the needs of families, strikes and demonstrations flourished. General strikes could cripple a city, with garbage piling up and transportation at a standstill. Even police officers went on strike in Boston, forcing the National Guard to restore order.

Workers weren't the only ones affected by the postwar economy. Industrialists in Waterbury had to find ways to keep people working and retool for a civilian economy. Not all companies were worried though. Scovill earned unprecedented profits during the war and used the healthy revenues to acquire its customers, a move that enabled the company to control more of the market. This was the period in which Scovill bought the Pin Company in Oakville. Other companies absorbed into Scovill were Hamilton Beach of Wisconsin and Gilchrist, a maker of soda fountain equipment.

Armed with a strong position in industry and financial security, Scovill weathered the Great Depression, as its company history states, "with its physical assets intact and its organization, seasoned by more than a century of business, relatively unscathed."

In 1937, workers fought for more money and benefits, scaring the brass industry into making concessions. A five-cent-per-hour increase was awarded to workers and vacation pay was implemented. The following year the awards were rescinded and wages were cut when an economic recession rocked the country. For average workers, the cuts were deep. In *Brass Valley*, author Jeremy Brecher writes that women were earning less than $5.50 a week for forty hours' work.

The old hope of having fragmented shops in larger industries as a buffer against widespread organization was challenged that year when the Mine Mill Union made its way into town.

A strike in Ansonia frightened the Waterbury industrialists, and they sought ways to counteract worker unrest with technological improvements that lessened the need for people. Not only the large companies were affected. Workers had struck in sympathy at Platt Brothers, a smaller firm, but the management there recognized it as ethnic solidarity rather than specific complaints. Always steadfast in their beliefs, the Platt family maintained a steady management style where everyone filled in for whatever need was presented. Workers were responsible for being flexible, meeting deadlines and producing high-quality work. Foremen were charged with properly training the workforce, coordinating production and helping with technological problems. Management's task was job security. This bolstered the employees' sense of engagement, which thwarted major labor unrest.

Platt Brothers and Patent Button, like other industries, took advantage of the war boom by producing fuses and buttons, and in the wake of that financially advantageous period, problematic changes came from both without and within. With their conservative management of the metalworking business, the Platts took advantage of the postwar years to stockpile raw materials and kept people working in any way they could without implementing restrictive practices that would lessen the feeling of independence their workers enjoyed.

The Platt Brothers operated on a smaller scale.

Unlike the conglomerates downtown, the Platt workers included family members and often several members of the same families. Many were gleaned from nearby farms that saw manufacturing as a secondary way to make money, and some even lived in the Platt boardinghouse.

Prior to the war's start, the Platt family essentially had two large businesses to run. Thomas Porter served as the company president for Patent Button and was a stockholder who wanted to venture into competing with the larger brass manufacturers. This directly defied the family precept set down by Alfred Platt and would siphon off resources from the metalworking business.

Reorganization had to occur, especially since a new generation of Platts was to take the helm. With the financial security and prosperity the Platt family members enjoyed, working for a dollar was not the impetus. Family members were also no longer farmers living next to their family factory. Lewis Platt spent part of his time developing a manufacturers' insurance cooperative and visiting his New York and Florida homes.

The family had diversified their stock portfolios and invested in real estate. Carrie Platt recalled earning $100,000 a year prior to World War I, with only half of that coming from manufacturing.

Family members pondered how to proceed after the war and decided that it might be wise to consolidate their efforts into one company. The Patent Button Company was reorganized in a way that left Porter with only 12.5 percent of the stock, and the enterprise was put on the market. A buyer soon emerged from Detroit by the name of Leonard Carley, who, as it turns out, could not come up with the financing.

Not to be dissuaded from a business he saw as having potential, Carley persuaded the Platts to take him on as a general manager in order to implement a plan for growth that included an aggressive sales strategy of employing salesmen with exclusive territories. Knowing that this would be a move contrary to the management plan Porter avowed—to acquire more competitors—the family moved to change the bylaws, creating a board of seven seats rather than four. This changed the makeup of the board from two Platt members and two Porter members to one in which six Platt members served alongside only one Porter.

The change allowed Porter to be eased out of the company without rancor and to continue following the plan for success laid out by Alfred Platt: to eschew quick profits in lieu of maintaining long-term continuity; to be a stable employer and supplier; to be reliable in all dealings; to maintain a paternalistic approach to management of people; and to maintain family participation in daily operations.

In the postwar years, new markets had to be forged by the Platts, and changes in old markets meant retooling to meet the need. Traditionally, the Platts produced zinc lace tips that were being replaced in the market with cheaper synthetic ones. One way to refortify the company's financial security in a changing market was to embrace electricity. With more homes and businesses being electrified, there was a growing need for fuses that would cut the current when a circuit was overloaded. Zinc was the main source of metal employed by the Platts and it proved to be exactly right for the job.

This change coincided with the change in management when Orton Camp Sr. assumed stewardship of the company in 1919. Camp was the son of Wallace Camp, who married into the Platt family. Camp was considered a mechanical genius and was responsible for taking the company out of the nineteenth-century model and into the twentieth-century model. Though his father, Wallace, and brother, Roland, had the title of president, it was Orton who had the vision and ran the show.

The money the family made during the war years was invested in improving the technology of the factory, and this growth didn't dissipate until the Great Depression. The result of that period left Orton Sr. with a great tendency toward conservatism in the latter part of his tenure.

Orton Camp Jr. told company biographer Matthew Roth, "My father had the belief that the company should not get any bigger than it was. He wanted a small company making specialty items for selected good customers." It followed Alfred Platt's belief that the company should never be so large that a family member lost control. Controlling the company with an eye toward job security for employees was a path to success.

Rather than strive to get bigger and bigger in order to attract some outside buyer, Orton Camp Sr. worked to keep his employees producing and to tackle new challenges. He also devoted his time to civic duties, sitting on the city's finance board and starting both the Waterbury Taxpayers' Association and the Naugatuck Valley Industrial Council.

Meanwhile, Carley's plan for Patent Button was paying off during the 1920s, when Waterbury's buttons fastened almost every pair of dungarees and overalls in America.

The Platt family's evolution had proceeded beyond the growth stage and into maintenance mode. Orton Camp Sr. from Platt Brothers and distant cousin David Hart ran the two companies and embodied the rift that had formed within the family. The Hart side of the family was larger and therefore provided more workers taking salaries. Both sides shared the stock equally. But the Hart clan also felt that the Camps wanted to take over the company.

Each company leader was able and, through their sons, planned to continue steering the family fortunes unscathed through another generation.

Orton Camp Jr. was educated at Yale, knowing that his career would be spent at Platt Brothers. Following his graduation, he joined and served in the Army Signal Corps until one day when his father took him to lunch at the Waterbury Club to meet a cousin he didn't know—David Hart from Patent Button. At that lunch, Hart wisely hired Orton Jr. as an accountant. In turn, Orton hired young Curtiss Hart as a bookkeeper at Platt Brothers. This was a move to begin reparations of the family breach.

Waterbury was a community with a diverse range of businesses. The common thread woven throughout all was success.

The Platt family was not the smallest of the manufacturers in the Naugatuck Valley. The wealth and bustle of this region attracted all sorts of individual entrepreneurs, none of whom gained more nostalgia appeal than Chief Two Moon Meridas.

His real name was Chico Colan Meridan and he was born in 1888 of uncertain lineage. Unlike most Waterbury citizens who enjoy tracing their family back, Chief Two Moon fostered an enigmatic persona.

Having arrived in town prior to World War I, he began selling medicinal elixirs—a common enough enterprise at a time when such remedies often contained alcohol or opiates. Chief Two Moon's recipe for his bitter oil contained none of that, relying on herbs, tincture of gentian, aloes and mineral oil. Meridas and his wife hawked the bottles of remedy anywhere they could—in parking lots, roadsides or from home.

The business got an unexpected boost when the influenza epidemic raced through town. Though Waterbury was hit hard with casualties, none of Chief Two Moon's patients contracted the disease and his fame spread. During the 1920s, his business prospered and grew, finally settling in a building on East Main Street that he adorned with Indian heads and two moons on the outside wall. Along with the East Main Street laboratory and store, the company had traveling buses and an airplane to distribute the "Wonder Tonic" throughout the United States and Europe.

Chief Two Moon adamantly purported to be of Indian descent, and in 1930 he was made an honorary chief by the Oglala Lakota tribe. His other honors included a meeting with the pope and civic receptions in New York City and Atlantic City.

Detractors, however, claimed that he wasn't Indian at all but was hiding a black lineage. Though lauded in New York, he was arrested and convicted for practicing medicine without a license. Connecticut, in turn, charged him with practicing naturopathy without a license. Despite the setbacks, Chief Two Moon gained wealth and spent some of it on needy neighbors in Waterbury.

In one case, a man did not know that he was an entrepreneur, but by the twentieth century his handicraft had become distinguished and, in modern times, very lucrative.

John W. Hill served in the Civil War, and following his discharge from the service, he entered the postal system. His tenure at the Waterbury Post Office and in the postal system spanned forty-three years, ending in 1918. He was born in Straitsville, Connecticut, in 1834, but his family moved to Waterbury to seek work. He earned the rank of corporal in Company E of the Sixth Connecticut Volunteer Infantry in 1861, and when he reenlisted after being disabled in the war, Hill was awarded the job of regimental postmaster.

His postwar postal duties included canceling stamped mail as it passed through the system. This was a time when "obliterators" were carved from cork and placed within a handle. As the cork wore, they would be tossed into the heating stove.

Hill rose above the others of his time. His designs were varied, amusing and true folk art gems. He had been an avid whittler, and the medium of cork beckoned him to create. There is one story that, while fishing, Hill amused himself by whittling a continuous chain out of a stick of pine. Once he whittled the bust of Grant for the top of a cane. It wasn't hard for those who knew him to believe that he'd spend his quiet times at work creating something with a knife. Soon, others in the Waterbury office copied Hill's example, and the mail coming through town became distinctive in America.

John P. Elton was among the first to save the "Waterburys," as the cancellations came to be called. The whimsical nature of the designs attracted him. Soon others were attracted as well.

Hill's repertoire included designs that were geometric, simple decorations, rosettes, leaves, animals and silhouettes of people. His "running chicken" earned the most fame when a cancelled envelope bearing a series of three topped $1 million at auction.

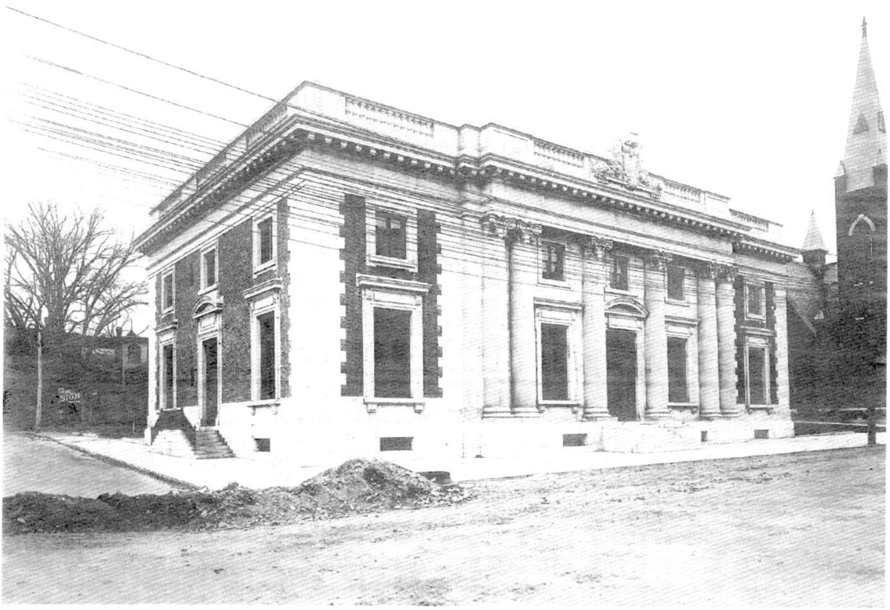

Waterbury Post Office
John Hill helped make Waterbury famous with his folk art cancellations, which are prized by collectors. *From the author's collection.*

Hill died in 1921, but before his death, collectors contacted him to glean information about the designs. They were simple explanations. For example, when his friend George did him a favor, Hill commemorated his gratitude with a letter *G* becoming the next Waterbury obliterator. When the Waterbury Excelsior baseball team beat the Naugatuck Valley Nine in 1867, the cancellation in the triumphant Waterbury was crossed baseballs and bats.

Today's collectors may not have access to Hill's memory, but there are several reference books dedicated to the Waterbury postmaster's designs. Counterfeits, unauthenticated cancellations and fancies add drama to the collecting, but as the values continually rose, the Waterbury cancellation disappeared from the general market.

Waterbury cancellations abounded for their time since Waterbury qualified as a full city that had more than $500,000 in postal receipts. By 1935, the population had risen to 100,000, and the city boasted three public high schools, thirty-four elementary schools, two parochial high schools, nine grammar schools, two business colleges and three private academies. A sum of $41 million was deposited in local banks, and Waterbury was second to Boston for outgoing freight. The retail sector served 200,000 people, as did the two hospitals (plus one isolation hospital for epidemics), and the library contained 150,000 volumes. Inhabitants received one Sunday paper and could choose any one of three local daily papers and a selection of weekly papers. Eleven fire stations protected Waterbury, as did the 170 police officers.

The year 1935 was an active one for the city. The factories were prosperous and the true level of Mayor Hayes's shenanigans hadn't yet come to light. Waterbury wanted to celebrate the end of the Great Depression by commemorating its past, and to this end a tercentenary festival was launched and a "Settlement" village was constructed in Chase Park.

The village highlighted the early living conditions of Waterbury's first families, but it also included representative scenes from various other groups. A stockade was erected, and within its confines a visitor could witness early American dwellings leading up to a central "Town Hall." One of the first structures encountered was the Indian longhouse, followed by a hunter's dugout. More permanent homes called "Agreement Houses" came next. These were wood houses, sixteen feet square, with a single room and fireplace. The substantial building material assured the state that the owners would remain in the area in order to secure a stable township. One of the most distinctive features of this was the oil coating on the exterior to repel water. Furniture within the Agreement House was crude and constructed for the festival by grade school children.

Farther along the festival route a visitor encounters the "Farmington House," which was patterned after the Whitman House in the Farmington Plantation. This early American construction is representative of the colonial period—a rectangular wooden structure of twenty by thirty-five feet fitted with a center chimney.

The largest house was the "Lean-to," a thirty-six-foot-square white clapboard house with interior rooms dedicated as exhibition space for smaller groups of inhabitants. Germans, Jews, blacks, Scandinavians and the Scottish were included.

An international section honored the many nationalities that composed the Waterbury citizenry. A thatched white cottage represented the Irish. The Italian house of stone sported a slate roof and tiled floors. The French style was distinctive in the steep roofline and stone walls. The Polish, Lithuanian and Russian houses were similar in design, each with a large warming oven. The Polish dwelling had dovetailed corners and a thatched roof. The Russian exterior was of logs.

Chapter Seven

WORLD WAR II

Waterbury's role in World War II is well documented in Ken Burns's recent documentary *The War*, which premiered on PBS in 2007. The premiere was held at the Palace Theater and the preliminary events were well attended by the people of Waterbury, some of whom remembered living during that time.

The Second World War, like the first, was a time of great production. History books cite that America's involvement began when Pearl Harbor was attacked in 1941. But Waterbury's contribution began long before this.

European rumblings started early in the 1930s while the Great Depression had a firm hold on the world's economy. But in 1939, Germany's military made a bold move by invading Poland, launching a war between two collective powers. Germany, Italy and Japan (the Axis Powers) launched a campaign against Great Britain and France, later adding the United States to the Allies in 1941.

Germany had suffered in the wake of World War I, and the citizens rallied around a charismatic young leader who promised them economic wealth and world leadership. A powerful army was forged, and it marched east into Poland and later west into Belgium and France. With most of Europe under its thumb, the Axis attacked London with an aerial blitzkrieg whose bombs devastated much of the city and terrorized the populace.

From 1939 to 1941, when America officially entered the fray, Waterbury's factories, like those in other cities, were manufacturing the products used in war. The intensive manufacture process honed during the earlier war helped in the retooling from peacetime to war production.

Mattatuck Manufacturing shifted from creating upholstery nails to cartridge clips, pumping out as many as three million a week. American Brass produced two billion pounds of brass rods, sheets and tubes. Chase contributed fifty million cartridge cases and mortar shells, one billion or more small caliber bullets and even some of the components for the atom bomb carried into Japan on the *Enola Gay*. Waterbury Clock Company produced fuses, and Scovill's inventory included a multitude of wares specifically done for the war.

America's entry into the war was not unexpected. Despite its neutral stance, the country supplied arms to the Allies through its lend-lease program, and the U.S. Navy was deployed to escort British ships across the Atlantic Ocean. Because of this, it was not unlikely that Germany would target U.S. industrial cities as potential targets for bombs.

Waterbury was on that list.

A shift had occurred in American cities. Workers had deep ties to their European homelands during the First World War. During the second, those ties were more closely bound to America and democracy. It was a fight to keep the world free of tyranny.

Factories went into high gear, running three shifts, and women filled in for the departing GIs. Waterbury sent 12,500 men and women into the Armed Forces.

At home, life went on, though a bit differently than before. One difference was a team of spotters stationed on the roof of city hall, searching the skies for German aircraft. The threat of attack was real enough that the Waterbury Watch Company transferred its production to a Middlebury plant built to camouflage the roof with water and *trompe l'oeil* trees to resemble a pond from the air.

The old Liberty House was reestablished and bonds were sold on the town green. Entertainments in town, including proms and other school events, were predominantly female. Everyone participated in the war effort. Goods were rationed and hardships were many, but the local people busied themselves by collecting more than 68,000 pounds of rubber, more than 5 million pounds of scrap metal, more than 8 million pounds of wastepaper and 150 tons of waste fat.

Those men unfit for duty supplied support work in any way they could to bring the war to a speedy end and ensure freedom for all people.

Young Vincent Codiani of Waterbury entered the army with that very intention. On Christmas Eve 1944, he was among more than two thousand soldiers heading across the English Channel toward the fight in France. The ship that carried them was the SS *Leopoldville*, a Belgian troopship bringing men for the upcoming Battle of the Bulge.

Five and a half miles outside of Cherbourg, France, the ship was hit by a German torpedo. Vinnie recalls being called to deck and all the men standing in their battle dress waiting to abandon ship.

"We were told to wait," Vinnie says. "Meanwhile the Belgians abandoned the ship and its passengers."

A British commander took control and dropped anchor to prevent the drift into a nearby minefield. The dropped anchor made it impossible for the rescue tug to haul the ship back to Britain.

The ship was in peril. "When the ship started to go down we were told to get off," Vinnie says. "Men jumped into the water. A lot of men died when they jumped. The water filled their helmets when they went into the water and snapped their necks."

Vinnie was lucky and survived the drop into the icy water. He was injured but alive, trying to stay afloat, waiting for help. Heavy seas and delayed radio transmissions hampered aid to the survivors, and the men watched helplessly as the *Leopoldville* sank beneath the waves two and a half hours after it was hit.

"It was a long night," Vinnie remembers. "I could barely feel my feet and I thought no one would come."

Approximately 2,235 American soldiers sailed on the *Leopoldville*, and of these, 763 never made it to shore. Many bodies were never recovered. Some drowned, some froze to death and some died in the fall.

Vinnie made it through, and after a period of recovery he joined the Allied forces in Europe.

"What got to me was that it was covered up," he remembers.

The incident of the *Leopoldville* was deemed classified until 1996 to cover up the embarrassing facts.

> *The governments didn't want people to know we'd been abandoned by our allies (the Belgians) and left to die. They didn't want the public to know about all the mistakes that were made. But a lot of people didn't know what happened to their loved ones.*

At the war's end, Vinnie remained in Europe and recalled the horrors of concentration camps. Most of the world shuddered at the news that the Axis, especially Germany, had employed slave labor and concentration camps of horrendous condition. Most alarming was the knowledge that Jews were being killed en masse and their bodies burned in a production line set to wipe out the entire race from the continent.

When surrenders were made, Waterbury and other American cities were left to retool and take steps into what would become a short period of plenty during the Cold War. And while the companies retooled, 10,200 workers lost their jobs.

Chapter Eight

POST WORLD WAR II

What happened to brass workers in the 1950s began in the economic recession of 1938, when the brass companies took back pay raises and vacation pay allocated the previous year. The discord among workers had reached a pitch that united the various component shops within the larger companies. The Mine Mill Union finally had its "hook" in Waterbury.

Making inroads in Waterbury wasn't easy for the labor organizers. The brass industries were broken into smaller, independent shops and the workers were fragmented along ethnic lines. No one trusted the other. Italians mistrusted the Irish for having choice jobs; English-speaking workers ignored European immigrants. And as far as the workers were concerned, things got worse when the companies hired southern blacks as strikebreakers. Discrimination was so rampant that it caused workers to overlook their similar problems.

With the Mine Mill Union negotiating contracts there was hope for a time of empowerment. That road to empowerment was anything but smooth. By 1941, deep divisions within the union were present, and the schism polarizing workers was communism.

The Red Scare had begun, and the American Communist Party, which had been a leader in the labor movement, was seen as too involved in policymaking. Workers in Waterbury began to feel unease because the issue at hand was American involvement in World War II. Prior to 1940, labor was not keen to become embroiled in Europe's turmoil, but by 1941 that agenda changed when the German army invaded Russia. Irish workers in Waterbury remained against involvement and felt that America's aid would directly benefit Britain. Deep resentments still festered with regard to the Great Famine and Ireland's independence.

By 1943 the Mine Mill Union in Connecticut was in disarray, culminating in the secession of some workers to the Provisional Metalworkers Council

(PMC). The fractionalization continued as PMC continued to raid Mine Mill for workers, forcing the two bitterly opposed unions to merge with larger entities—the PMC joined with the United Auto Workers (UAW) in 1950 and Mine Mill became part of the Steelworkers Union in 1960.

The years following World War II were ones of growth. A boom in births was expected, and that meant the city had to look to increasing the number of schools and providing housing for returning GIs. Almost overnight, the old structures of American life gave way to a new prosperity. Homes were erected on the outskirts of towns, in outlying regions that were quickly becoming suburbs. Personal transportation allowed workers to move families to more bucolic settings, abandoning the congestion of urban neighborhoods.

It was a sea change for the country. Until this period, people had lived primarily in cities, in a communal setting where neighbors lived close to one another (sometimes as few as ten feet apart) and recreated together in movie houses, theaters and at parks. Children walked en masse to school, and shopping was within walking distance. If someone had to travel across town, the bus provided transportation. There was a sense of continual contact with people. The move outward from the cities created a different way of existing. Homes were surrounded by lawns, and because of the plentitude of automobiles acquired by consumers, shopping was a distance away in places that accommodated parking. Sidewalks became extraneous and children rode buses to school. Television made the trip to the movies less routine. Americans were becoming increasingly isolated in modern homes that were more transitional in nature.

Being able to afford this lifestyle and to ensure its continuation led workers to seek more money and benefits. It wasn't surprising, then, when a major strike closed Waterbury factories in 1952.

What made this strike different from the one in 1920 was a change in workers' rights. In 1920, the industry owners could employ the police and National Guard as strikebreakers. Management could ignore worker complaints because it felt secure that the unions were somewhat disorganized due to worker differences and factories being fractured into smaller shops.

By 1952, this had changed. The American government now allowed workers to organize and protected their rights to bargain with management. They could now picket without fear of reprisal. Unions had evolved and become more efficient. Most importantly, workers had become more "Americanized" by sharing the same language, sending their children to the same schools and living among their fellow workers of diverse ethnic descent.

The World War II profits did not mean an easy switch to peacetime production for the brass industry because plastic and aluminum had become a product of choice in the marketplace. As a result, a decision was made not to retool as they had in the past. Profit reinvestment went elsewhere, where labor was cheap and construction of new, more efficient factories was more affordable. The behemoth plants that had so great a footprint in Waterbury began to crumble and then to move out. Like a snake shedding its skin, companies slipped away from the valley, leaving the outer layer behind to rot.

Yet, immigrant workers continued to arrive. There was a postwar wave from Italy and Portugal and a new flow of people from Puerto Rico. These newcomers found themselves in a different position than the earlier immigrants in town.

First, there were no jobs to readily employ them. Second, the "Americanized" immigrants saw them as being "off the boat." The support system in place for larger groups had become obsolete. It was up to the newly arrived to find their own way in a difficult transition period. The Cold War and Red Scare encouraged a movement to Americanize. Ethnicity was discouraged.

The story of Erminia Ciriello is not atypical. After finishing school in an Italian convent, she joined her mother and brother onboard a ship headed for what they called "Mattaburg." The economy in their hilltop town of Ginestra was stagnant, and relatives in Waterbury seemed to have more promising futures.

The city seemed ideal, with its deep-rooted Italian community and plethora of Catholic churches.

Work and living were foremost in the Ciriello family's mind. Their first apartment was on Orange Street, an easy walk to the brass company where Luigi Ciriello found employment and the garment factory where Erminia and her mother, Maria, could ply their sewing skills. With piecework added to a regular pay, their industry earned them the hope that a house of their own was within reach. English classes provided the two youngsters the opportunity to "fit in" more quickly.

Both Erminia and her brother married and bought homes in the Bucks Hill area—small houses with plenty of grass and nearby farms that were perfect for raising a family. Erminia bore five children; Luigi (Lou) had two.

The turbulent years of the 1960s' protests seemed to pass over the family, but the 1970s brought changes that would reshape their lives. A large subdivision cropped up where fields once lay. The brass mills had departed, and unemployment had risen to more than 15 percent in Waterbury. Job security was at an all-time low and inflation was at an all-time high.

But because of her frugality, Erminia Ciriello (now Gaeta) was able make a bold leap, and she moved her family to the Overlook neighborhood.

The Columbia Boulevard area was a bastion of Irish and Jewish professionals—doctors, lawyers and business owners. The rising cost of heating oil caused many of these families to rethink whether the cost of maintaining a near-mansion-size house was practical. Encroachment from nearby minority groups (more specifically, when the Pearl Street Neighborhood Association relocated to Columbia Boulevard) opened up property at an affordable price, allowing new groups of working-class people to buy in.

The Gaetas soon were ensconced in a fifteen-room home of Mediterranean style, surrounded by a formal garden. Inside, the difference was enormous between the new home built prior to World War I and their newer, small Cape on Bucks Hill.

Dan Gaeta, Erminia's oldest son, recalled the family's move. The house had plenty of room for everybody, including his grandmother, Maria, who helped with childcare. The rooms were spacious and filled with thick oak molding. The plaster walls and heavy doors kept noise to a minimum. Rooms on the main floor were kept private by beveled glass-paned French doors equipped with beautiful brass hardware. The dining room contained a crystal chandelier. The large staircase window was of leaded glass.

Their former neighbors had been farmers and factory workers (like Dan's dad, Rocco Gaeta). The new neighbors included physicians, teachers, a state representative and dentists. But this move did not insulate the family from the economic hardships of this period. What was costly for the previous owners proved equally costly for the Gaetas. Heating a house of that size was a challenge, one that they met in the same way their neighbors were trying to cope. Alternative or zoned heating was created by creative means. Downstairs rooms were closed off to keep the heat in. The kitchen served as the central gathering place, and something was always baking in the oven. Heat was provided for upstairs by a kerosene heater placed in the central hall. Later, a wood-burning stove was installed in the living room fireplace.

Dan jokes that their attic became a museum of space heaters.

More markedly, the family's changes were twofold. Factory work in Waterbury became precarious, and Erminia enrolled in the local community college to "retool." This was at a time when her own children were heading into higher education. While Erminia studied to become a recreational therapist in a nursing home (geriatrics being deemed an area of growth), her children Mary Lou, Dan, Michael and Diana were heading off to college. Two left the state, while the other two enrolled in state colleges.

Lou Ciriello, meanwhile, found himself in the precarious position of keeping himself working within the dwindling brass industry. Erminia's short stint as a therapist hit the same kind of roadblock—a pension would not be forthcoming.

This was an abrupt change for Waterbury workers. Previous generations had enjoyed job security. Many men entered a factory and retired from it.

As a consequence, Erminia was forced back into school to obtain a bachelor's degree in social work, eventually landing a state job in the Labor Department. It took three jobs and two degrees to guarantee her old age with a pension.

Her children were like other college-educated youngsters from the area and ended up finding jobs out of state. Mary Lou opted to study medicine and worked in New York City before taking a job at Yale and later becoming the pediatric hospitalist at Bridgeport Hospital. Michael finished UConn and went to San Francisco to study podiatry before moving to a practice in Seattle. Diana ended her classes at Southern Connecticut State University and found employment in the airline industry in Houston. Only Dan returned from his studies at NYU to work locally, opening a business in downtown Waterbury.

Other immigrants, like Erminia, found life less abundant in Waterbury. Puerto Ricans coming to Waterbury found the unskilled work market very lean. A vibrant community of Puerto Ricans had developed in the South End, and a small business community had begun to thrive, but when urban renewal came to Waterbury, the South End suffered.

A major interstate highway bisected the city east to west when I-84 was constructed. The South End was cut off from the central business district, keeping the economic market localized in the nearby neighborhood. As a consequence, those who could afford to move did so. Businesses could not grow and opportunities waned. The neighborhood became a slum. Some of the nearby factories were abandoned, creating large pockets of blight and pollution and making it nearly impossible to revitalize.

By the 1980s, only a few brass plants were left, and these were employing a tiny fraction of the Waterbury labor market. Those still working in the industry faced the lack of a cohesive internal structure within the plant, the decline of the union's power and a bleak future.

The large brass companies were now conglomerates with business ties elsewhere. A second strike in 1956 lasted months, and owners pointed to this as an excuse to leave, claiming that workers were greedy.

The real reason for the exodus was that other areas were beckoning. The Sun Belt promised a cheaper cost of living for workers and more pleasant weather. Foreign countries promised three highly attractive incentives: very cheap labor (workers could be paid as little as $1.50 an hour), lots of empty land for expanding factories and few environmental controls.

The beginning of the economic downturn precipitated other problems within the city. People without work ended up on a growing welfare system. This left able-bodied people on a path that did not include home ownership or make them serious participants in the burgeoning consumer economy.

Frustration within the black community came to a head in 1969. The neighborhood of the North End was deteriorating, and Waterbury's black population was faced with discrimination at every level. A riot began after civil rights leader Dr. Martin Luther King Jr. was assassinated. The North End began to burn.

After the riot was quelled, the burned area was not rebuilt to include better housing or jobs—the empty space became parking lots, a park, a housing project and a social welfare agency. That entire section of the city was in decline.

Urban renewal became a mixed blessing for the city. The interstate that cut into the downtown did not bring in shoppers from the outlying regions. Instead, it made it easier to leave Waterbury. Malls and plazas along "miracle miles" were established elsewhere, supplanting the pedestrian-friendly downtown area where people used to converge when schools and factories poured citizens past local stores.

Urban renewal in downtown began with a clearing away of older buildings to make way for larger structures of a modern, concrete construction. Waterbury merchants objected to the wholesale bulldozing.

Some of downtown was architecturally important and the merchants launched a suit to save it. They won, but the mercantile area was in a decline that didn't stop. Without the factories and schools providing a steady stream of customers, storeowners began to feel a pinch. Over the years there have been promises and plans, but without downtown workers, many of the shops closed.

Malls proved the death knell for downtown retail. Waterbury's first mall was constructed in an unlikely spot, far from the highway near the Wolcott border. Leading to the site were newly constructed plazas that offered single-level construction and plenty of parking in front.

Downtown embarked on a plan to modernize. With American families now owning one, if not two, cars, parking seemed key to their future success. With a limited amount of land available in the congested central business district, ramp garages were constructed, multistoried structures designed to warehouse cars for short periods of time.

Unlike the free open lots in plazas, the parking garages were designed as a revenue stream for cities, much as parking meters had been.

People seemed to prefer the malls with free parking, and the downtown inventory of stores changed from long-established names to new, inexpensive bodegas.

Serious attempts were made by the state to salvage Waterbury's dwindling brass market by helping new companies willing to take over from the old. Century Brass moved in, but its tenure was short-lived. Older workers were suddenly thrust into the job market.

This period of transition was met educationally by a community college system developed in the late 1960s. Mattatuck Community College began with a hodgepodge of borrowed classrooms from high schools and empty buildings before constructing a campus on Chase Parkway. Returning Vietnam vets and displaced workers were able to receive an affordable education that allowed them to reenter a changing job market.

Classes in liberal arts and sciences were coupled with programs designed to put people back to work—much as they had for Erminia Gaeta. Nursing, social work, radiology and accounting were some of the courses that were often paid with federal student loans.

As Waterbury's economy languished, the college added service sector skills like automotive technology and culinary arts to the mix.

Chapter Nine

THE FLOOD OF 1955

The flood of 1955 was the one event that defined calamity for the city, as well as elsewhere in the state. It began with rain that fell in torrents after Hurricanes Connie and Diane moved up the Atlantic seaboard. On August 13, Connie moved inland through New Jersey and Pennsylvania toward the Great Lakes, changing the nature of the storm from high winds to a steady downpour that soaked the ground. It had been a wet summer. When Hurricane Diane clipped through on the eighteenth, that storm dumped fourteen inches of rain onto saturated soil.

For those in Waterbury, the rain failed to dampen the mood as local film star Rosalind Russell premiered her latest movie, *The Girl Rush*.

For thirty hours, from Thursday morning to Friday noon, the rain was unabated. With the ground filled with millions of gallons of rainwater and no hope of absorbing more, the water poured into streams and rivers, surging forward from Winsted to Seymour with a forceful push that resulted in widespread devastation.

Those living in Waterbury along the Naugatuck River floodplain, predominantly in the Brooklyn and South End neighborhoods, were hit the hardest. Homes splintered apart, brick factories were filled with silt and fast-moving debris that included entire trees pushed forward with relentless energy.

Waterbury Petroleum Company's multi-ton tanks were dislodged and floated downriver, crashing into buildings, spilling their contents and fouling the water. The Scovill Co. railroad trestle was swept away, and water rose along Freight Street until it reached the traffic lights. Waterville looked as if a large lake had formed in its midst.

Mel Bergin remembers her father taking her to work at American Brass. "We got to the bottom of Willow Street and we knew something was wrong," she remembered. Water covered the streets. The pair retreated to the top of

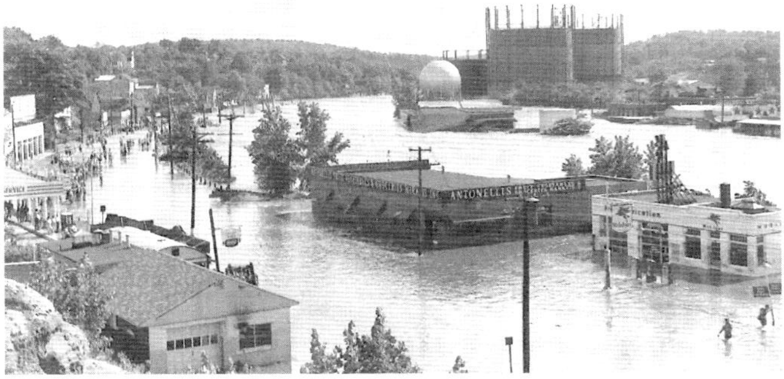

FLOOD SCENE
The Naugatuck River washed over its banks, putting parts of the city underwater. *From the author's collection.*

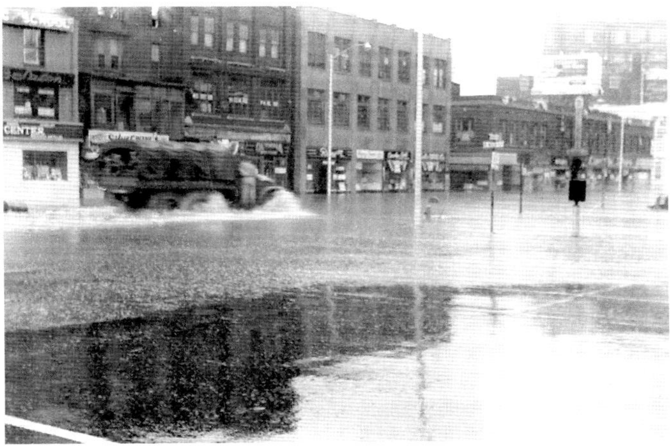

FLOOD SCENE, WEST MAIN STREET
People on their way to work were surprised to find downtown underwater. *From the author's collection.*

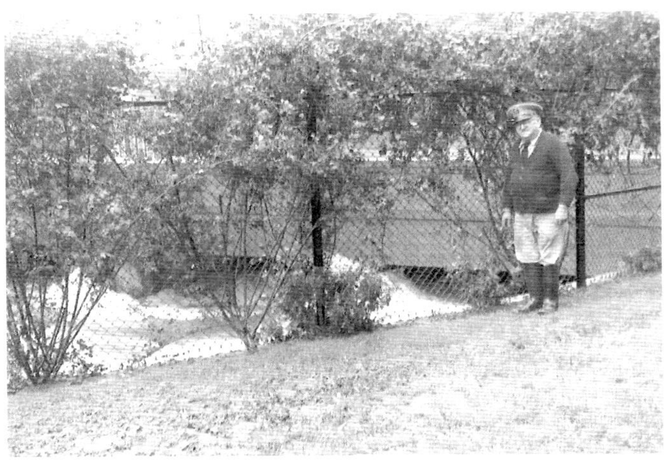

RUSH OF WATER
When the dam burst north of Torrington, Waterbury and the lower valley towns suffered an onslaught of water. *From the author's collection.*

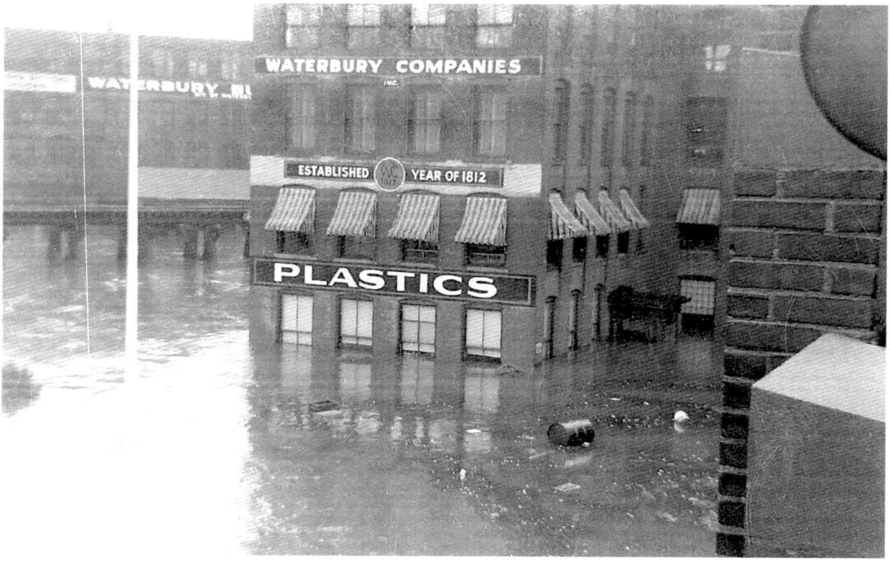

Flood Scene
On South Main Street the water rose from both sides of the Waterbury Company's Plastics Department. The Mad River runs alongside and the Naugatuck is half a block to the west. *From the author's collection.*

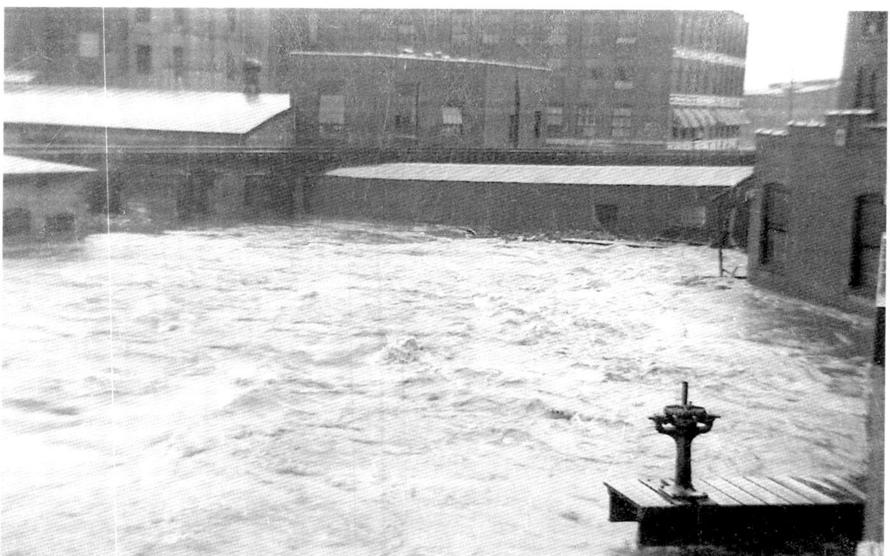

Mad River
The Mad River rose like the others and contributed to the deep water filling the center of the town. *From the author's collection.*

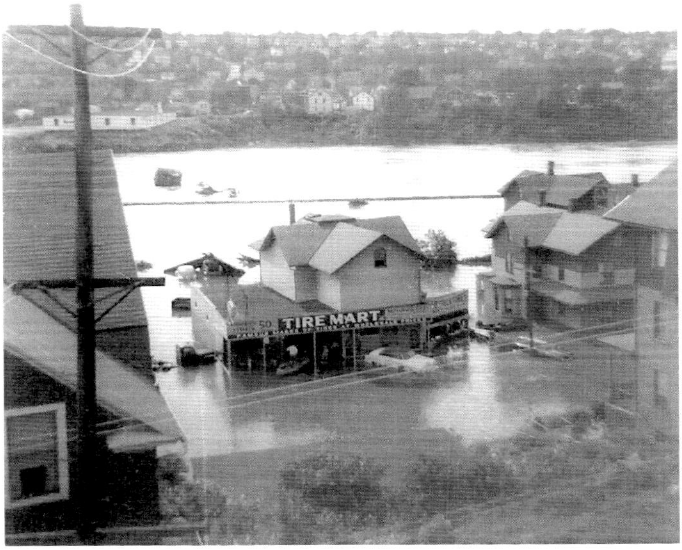

FLOOD, TIRE MART
Small businesses like the Tire Mart weathered the rising water but were still in danger. *From the author's collection.*

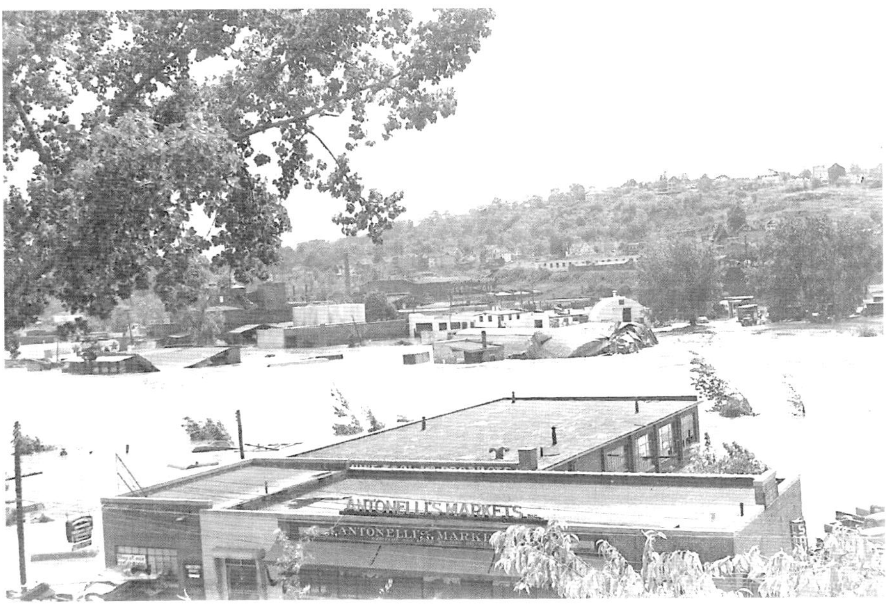

FLOOD, ANTONELLI'S
Antonelli's market originally stood on South Main Street and fell victim to the flood. Today, the market is in a warehouse on Freight Street. *From the author's collection.*

the hill and looked out over the river. "The water was high and then we saw a wave of water push down the river. There were three-family houses floating along with people on the roof. I don't know how they were saved."

American Brass was closed for three days, and when it reopened, Mel said, "Everything had a film of dirt on it. We had just gotten the Anaconda books and many people still had them in their desks. They literally crumbled in the water."

When the sun finally broke through that Friday afternoon, residents overlooking the valley from the east and west hills were stunned at the scope of the disaster. Rescues began immediately. The National Guard was mobilized by Governor Abraham Ribicoff to keep order and assist with the rescues. Sikorsky helicopters (including two that were slated for the Royal Canadian Air Force) were deployed and rescued 451 individuals stranded on rooftops.

The rescue missions weren't without mishap. A Coast Guard helicopter was assigned to evacuate stranded Chase Metal Works employees. While landing on the roof, the copter's tail crashed into a smokestack, causing the pilot and copilot to be transported to St. Mary's Hospital.

In all, six to seven hundred persons were airlifted to safety in the Naugatuck Valley.

Not everyone was patient about waiting. One unlucky Chase worker decided to brave the walk home and was caught in the rising water. Alvin Sparkman found himself adrift, being scratched and buffeted by tree limbs and debris. He endured a grueling two-mile swim to safety.

Schools were opened to house evacuees, and hospitals braced for an onslaught of injuries. The Red Cross began to feed the homeless and help families recover. Immunization shots to prevent diseases like cholera and typhoid were administered.

At 9:00 p.m., Chief Inspector Joseph Bendler was notified that the Torrington Dam had broken and the river was expected to rise fifteen feet. The National Guard estimated the rise to be only two feet, but volunteers began a house-to-house search for residents on North and South Leonard Streets, Bank Street and other low-lying lanes in order to evacuate them to St. Joseph's Hall. Some had evacuated earlier and willingly left their homes; others were forcibly removed for their own safety.

Volunteers along the river reported being beleaguered by river rats. Rescue vehicles caught in the flood were abandoned. One eighty-five-foot fire ladder was used to bridge the water in an attempt to rescue stranded people. When it fell short, a sixteen-foot ladder was added to reach a tenement. As the stranded inched to safety, the ladder twisted and dropped

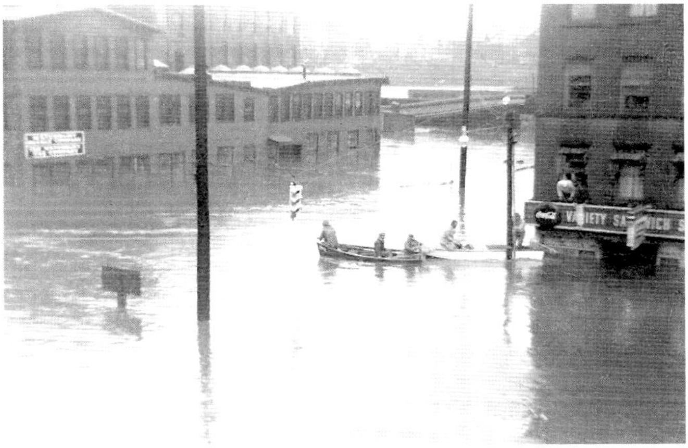

BOAT RESCUE
Rowboats were employed to rescue those remaining in their homes. *From the author's collection.*

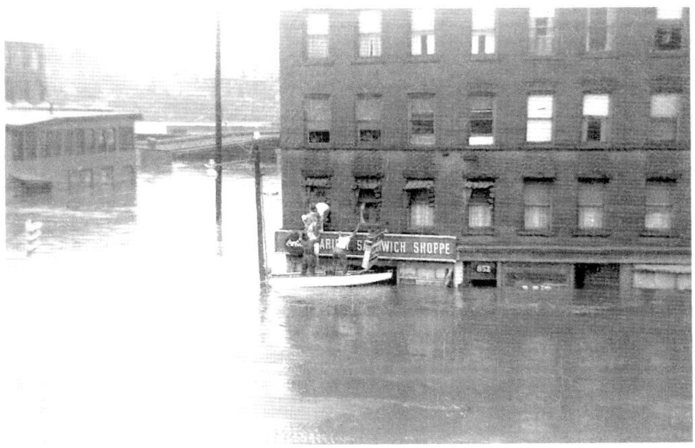

BOAT RESCUE
People are lowered into the boats from an upper-story window. *From the author's collection.*

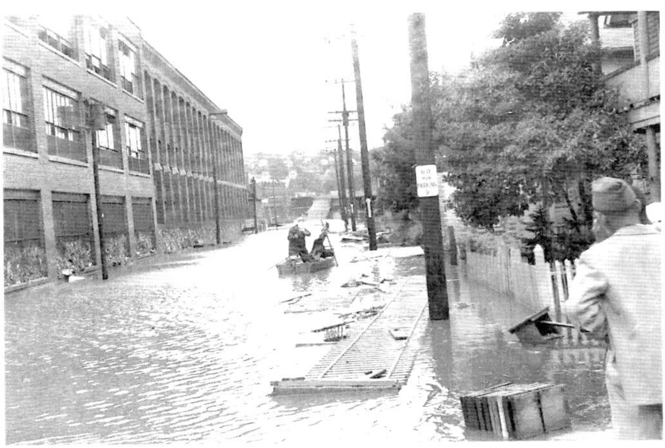

BOAT RESCUE
Nearly every street was traversed in the search for people. *From the author's collection.*

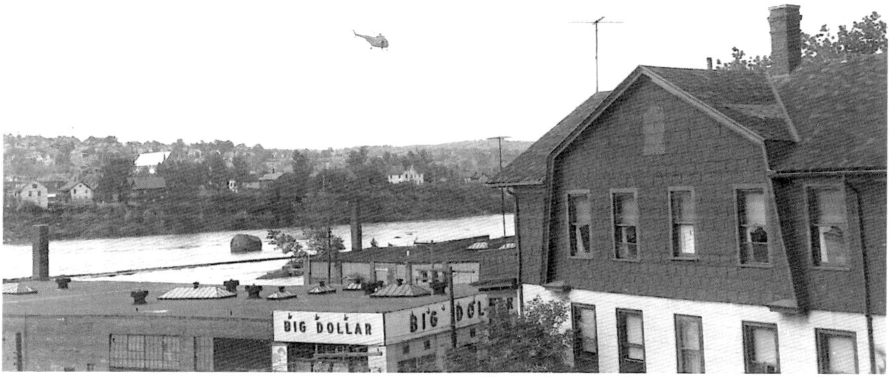

Helicopter
Sikorsky lent helicopters to aid in the rescue of hundreds of people that day. *From the author's collection.*

several people into the water, including a baby girl who was swept away. One fireman bravely tried to reach the girl but lost her after coursing downriver one hundred feet.

Putting the town back together wasn't going to be easy. The local paper was reporting that 115 residents had been injured and that housing the homeless had paralyzed facilities. Reporters were calling this disaster worse than the 1902 fire that destroyed downtown Waterbury. The water finally began to recede at a rate of six inches per hour.

Antibiotics were in short supply, and medical examiner Dr. Edward Kirschbaum put out a call to pharmacies to send medicines to Russell School and Waterbury Hospital.

Power was out everywhere, and the city had to rely on mobile generators to supply power to city hall and Plymouth Airport in order to keep radio transmitters working through the search and rescue operations.

Looters took advantage of the plight, and seventeen arrests were reported citywide. Prices for food rose. Milk and water were in such short supply that people lined up at the local Coca-Cola plant for soda. Dry ice was transported from New Haven by the state police to protect Waterbury's blood supply. The New England Telephone Company loaned the hospital a portable generator to be used along with the hospital's own to furnish power throughout the emergency. In order to make use of the generator, Scovill supplied three hundred feet of wire, which was rushed across town via a navy helicopter.

President Eisenhower declared the state a disaster area.

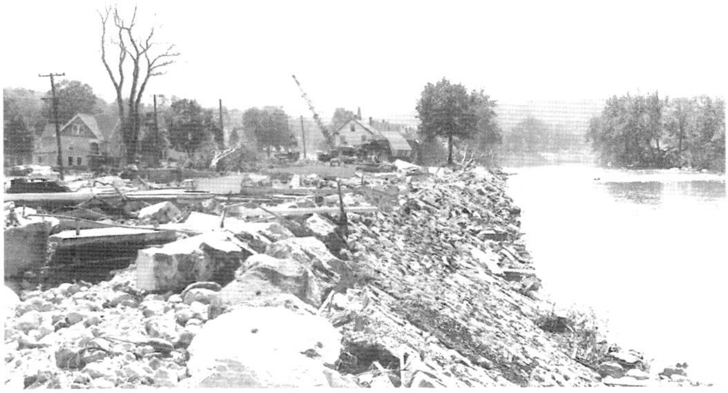

Wrecked House
Homes along South Main Street and in Brooklyn were wrested from their foundations. *From the author's collection.*

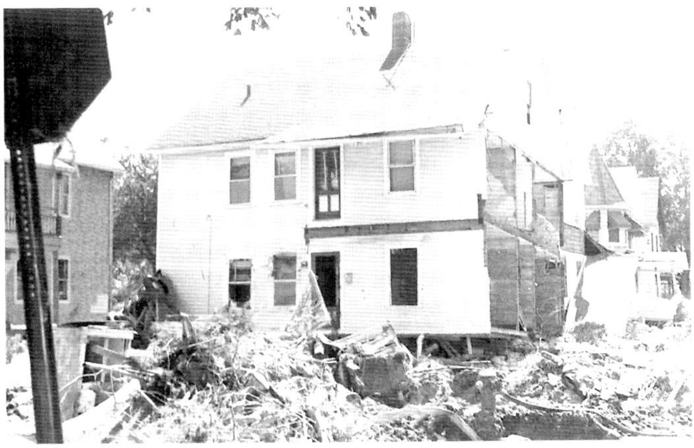

Wrecked House
People were rendered homeless. *From the author's collection.*

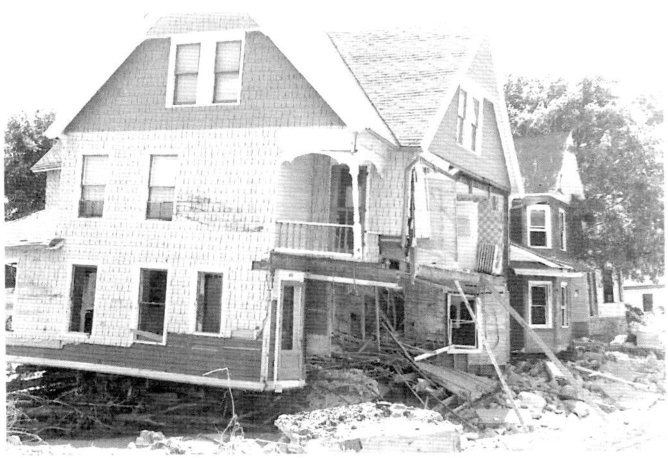

Wrecked House
What had seemed so permanent to families was now nothing more than junk. *From the author's collection.*

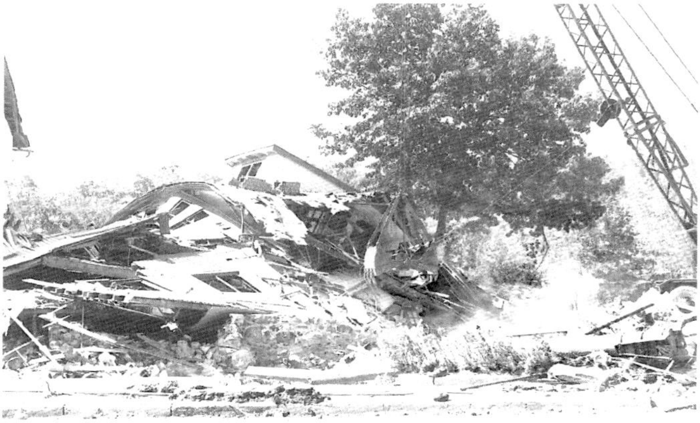

Wrecked House
Throughout the summer and into the fall, the city worked to clear the homes lost in the flood. *From the author's collection.*

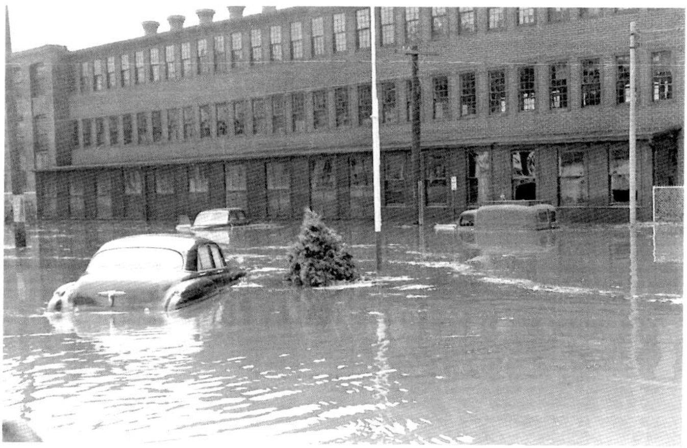

Flooded Factory
This factory on South Main Street was one of many that floodwaters filled with mud and debris. *From the author's collection.*

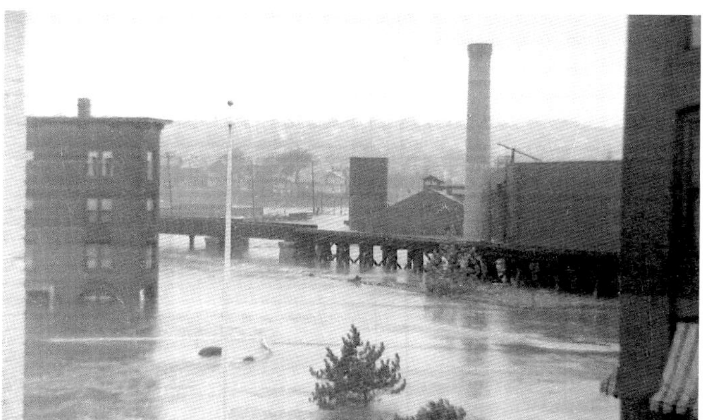

Flooded Factory
The final tally of losses reached into the millions. *From the author's collection.*

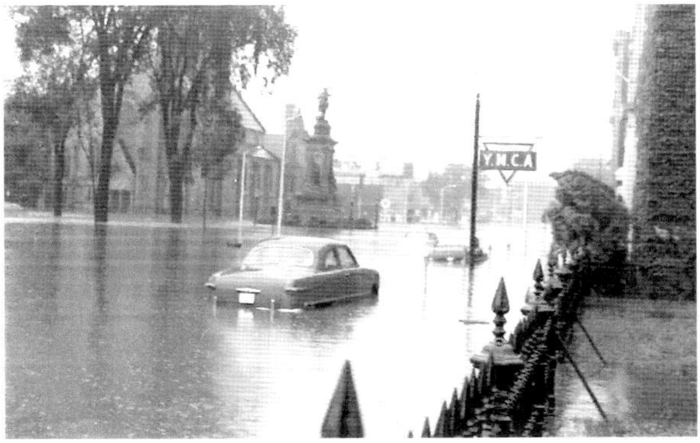

YMCA AND FLOODED DOWNTOWN
Looking westward from the YMCA, the car before the Soldiers' Monument shows how deep the waters rose on the green. *From the author's collection.*

The city went to work quickly and began to shore up its sanitation and public services, while business owners hired crews to help shovel away the silt that filled building interiors with mud and debris. Collapsed buildings had to be demolished, and the wreckage strewn along the river's shores needed to be carted away.

Governor Ribicoff reported the damages to 137 companies as exceeding $31 million. Waterbury's municipal loss was over $39 million. The newspaper reported the overall loss at $150 million, and the local citizens found dead numbered twenty-four. Seventeen residences were leveled.

John Moriarty was eight years old in 1955 and remembers that his father was the one to tell him about the catastrophe:

> *I was surprised when my father wasn't in work. He told me they were sent home because of a flood. Later, my grandparents took me down Faber Street where we lived and we could see all the water. Behind the Chase factory there were train trestles that were twisted like ribbon candy.*

When the water receded, the Moriarty family walked along Thomaston Avenue:

> *We weren't even thinking about cholera then, we just wanted to see what happened. The Ville Theater was open and we looked in. The seats were covered up to their backs in mud. My grandmother said, "remember this day your whole life."*
>
> *I never forgot it.*

For people in town, the flood became a touchstone—and memories are often prefaced with "before the flood" or "after the flood."

Chapter Ten

RELIGION

The preponderance of Waterbury residents belong to the Roman Catholic Church, but that wasn't always the case. The earliest settlers were Protestant and wanted the New World to be a place where they could live a life dedicated to God and simple worship. As the plantations settled into townships and roads began connecting communities, the land's resources beckoned more people to America who didn't share Puritan worship.

It was religion that formed the foundation of the city's social fabric and provided the disparate settlers with a common identity and purpose.

Within the Protest faith are a spectrum of sects that include the Church of England (Episcopals), Congregationalists (former Puritans), Methodists, Baptists and more. Waterbury had representatives from each sect and congregations grew. With the prosperity that time brought, the congregations began erecting substantial buildings in which to worship and to advertise their presence.

That group of churches is outnumbered by those built by the city's Catholics. What distinguishes the Roman Catholic Church in Waterbury has changed over history. At first it was a wellspring for producing priests; today it is the array of churches, each of which bears a distinct style.

A walk during Christmas illustrates the city's religious roots. If you start at the green, you will notice the crèche and menorah illuminated by the twinkling lights strung through trees. To the north sits the stately white marble Basilica of the Immaculate Conception, which boasts of its past in the beautifully polished brass accoutrements adorning the Italianate architecture. Within the church an ornate ceiling that was recently restored mantles the opulent setting.

To the west of the green is the more modern Congregational church, whose basement is utilized for a variety of community services. The large wing used for gatherings extends eastward, and the outside lawn hosts barbecues during the summer.

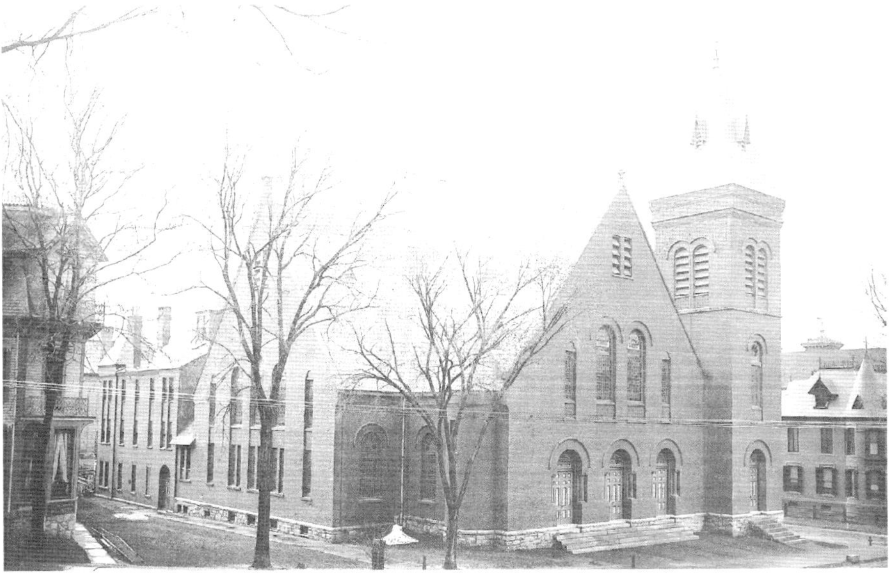

Methodist Episcopal Church
Within the population of Protestants in Waterbury, varying divisions produced thriving congregations. *From* Waterbury and Her Industries.

St. John's Church is reminiscent of an English county parish with its heavy stone architecture and single steeple. A stone addition serves as a social place for the members and a soup kitchen for the poor. The site has two distinctive elements. One is a quiet "close" surrounded by a wall that provides a leafy respite from the bustle of the city outside. The second feature is the stained-glass rose window that provides a welcoming visage.

Tucked behind the Immaculate is the old Trinity Church. At one time, the older Yankee population had enough Protestant members to warrant a second congregation downtown. With those numbers dwindling, the Trinity was dismantled and sold to the Immaculate for use as a day-care facility.

Moving south from the green, one sees the beautiful rising pair of steeples that marks St. Anne's, originally home to French Canadian Catholics. The building beside the church has been closed as a parochial school for a number of years but has served the city as a center for adult education. St. Anne's is now home to the Hispanic population along the South Main Street corridor and has been reinvented into a Shrine to Motherhood, producing musical programs that highlight sacred music of the highest caliber. It has plans to implement a community revitalization program to reclaim severely blighted property.

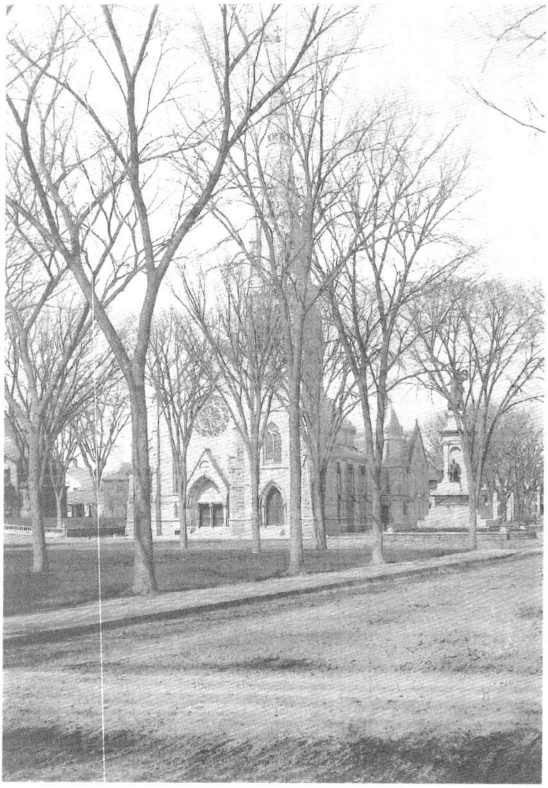

Left: St. John's
St. John's on the Green boasts an English style. The rose window, when illuminated at night, provides a peaceful beauty. *From* Waterbury and Her Industries.

Below: Trinity Episcopal
Trinity Episcopal was built to house the overflow of congregants from St. John's. At the time of its construction, it was a parish wealthy enough to include Tiffany windows. Today it is owned by the Basilica of the Immaculate Conception and is used as a day care. *From* Waterbury and Her Industries.

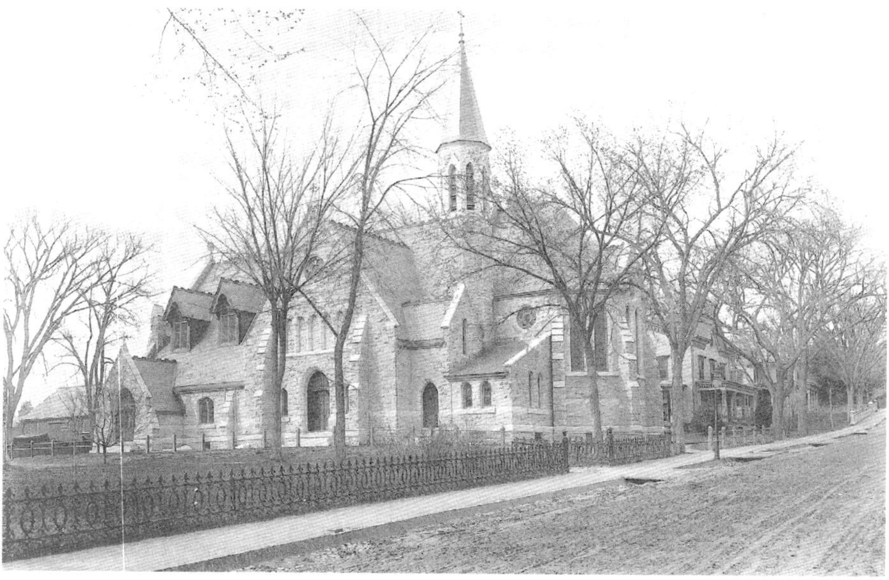

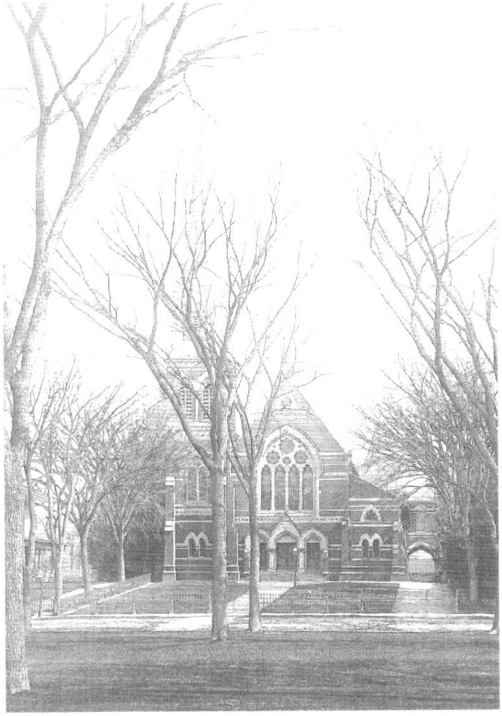

First Congregational Church
The First Congregational had a prominent place on Waterbury's green. Today this structure is a memory. The current Congregational church is farther west and is of a modern design. *From* Waterbury and Her Industries.

Before one reaches St. Anne's, one passes Our Lady of Lourdes Church, precariously nestled against the I-84 corridor. When the highway was built in the 1960s, it ran so close to the church that the structure had to be protected by a large wooden fence bordering the road. A visit inside the church reveals the true gem—a natural grotto sits beneath the altar.

Though the cross on the hill (illuminated at night so you don't miss it) proclaims Waterbury's Christian base, the religious population of the city is diverse and is represented by Hindu temples, synagogues, mosques and Mormon temples, as well as other houses of worship. Waterbury is a religious city and it is a tolerant one. While many communities bicker during the Christmas season over disallowing a crèche to be displayed on public property, Waterbury expands the season by including a menorah on the green.

It is a city where most of the immigrant ancestors were once sorely needed but whose presence was disdained. Inclusion seems to be the bedrock that forms this modern community.

The deep sense of religion was one reason why Communism failed to gain a strong foothold in the city, despite the large number of laborers hailing from Eastern European countries. Atheism had no role in town, and the

Catholic Church urged its Irish and Italian parishioners to forgo following a godless doctrine. It was advice that Waterbury heeded, given the great power wielded by the Catholics of this city.

The Catholic Church was not beyond meddling in politics to achieve its ends. During the 1930s, it launched a campaign against birth control that led to court. In his book *Liberty & Sexuality*, author David Garrow devotes an entire chapter to how the roots of *Roe v. Wade* took hold in Waterbury.

When the *Waterbury Democrat*, the town's more liberal paper, announced the opening of a birth control clinic, Catholic priests argued, in print, that they viewed birth control as a crime not dissimilar to illegal gambling.

When the Chase Dispensary allowed the Connecticut Birth Control League to use a consultation room in order to educate workingwomen about the use of contraception, the Catholic Church demanded that Catholic politicians eradicate the practice. It became a tussle between well-intentioned Protestant women, whose husbands controlled the industries in town, and the Roman Catholic Church, which had sway over the laborers and city workers alike.

Doctors viewed the interference of the Catholic Church as more than meddlesome. They signed a petition to persuade the court that the church had no right to interfere with medical practices. Church officials responded by firing doctors at St. Mary's Hospital who had signed this same petition.

In the end, it was the law that decided. By 1947, things hadn't changed much according to a report in *Time* magazine. A sixty-eight-year-old blue law in Connecticut continued to make it a misdemeanor for a doctor to advise, or a citizen to practice, birth control. Though it is seldom enforced, doctors periodically tried eleven different times to repeal it. Ironically, the legislator responsible for such a law was P.T. Barnum, a man seldom thought of as a bastion of propriety.

The next time the Catholic Church involved itself in secular matters was during the infighting of the Mine Mill Union. Irish workers objected to the union's policymaking being written by Communists, and they turned to their local priests for help. Church officials responded with classes to teach the Catholic laborers how to shape their union.

The highlight of Catholic history in Waterbury is yet to come. Local boy turned priest Father Michael J. McGivney is on track to become a saint—the city's first.

McGivney was born in 1852, as Waterbury began its peak years. He was the eldest of twelve children of Irish immigrant parents and was educated in the basement of St. Peter Church under the tutelage of Father Thomas Hendricken.

He was a good, knowledgeable student, but at age fourteen he took a three-year sabbatical from his studies to work in the brass mills, after which he entered the Seminary of St. Hyacinthe, run by the Jesuits. With his two sisters contributing to the family's income, McGivney was able to finish his theological training in Baltimore and was ordained on Christmas Eve 1877.

On Christmas Day, the young priest celebrated his first mass at the Immaculate Conception Church in front of family and friends. His first posting as an associate pastor was nearby, at St. Mary's in New Haven.

McGivney's experience as a laborer and living in a city filled with workers taught him two important life lessons—drunkenness was evil, and financial security was precarious for the laboring class.

To address the first, McGivney preached temperance and instituted recreations within his parish that didn't include alcohol, later forming the St. Joseph's Total Abstinence and Literary Society.

The priest had seen the rise of fraternal orders in cities, and though he abhorred their use of alcohol, he admired the insurance policies they provided for families. These societies were not open to Catholics, and McGivney hit upon the idea of forming his own that was loyal to America and provided assistance to families in need.

On March 29, 1882, the Knights of Columbus was recognized as an organization by the State of Connecticut.

McGivney had only a handful of years left to serve the church on this earth. He was posted to St. Thomas parish in Thomaston, where he died from pneumonia following a bout of flu in 1890.

Waterbury commemorated the priest's contribution to America and his fellow Catholics by erecting a statue in his honor, directly across from the train station at the very beginning of the "Grand Street." That street bears a second name now, Father McGivney Boulevard. He faces the city where the churches stand and where people live, and on March 15, 2008, Pope Benedict XVI declared this priest "Venerable," the first step toward canonization.

It is impossible to overlook the Russian Orthodox Church of St. Mary's. Russians migrated to Waterbury during the late nineteenth century, forming two religious groups in town. In 1906, those groups joined to plan for the formation of an official church on Crown Street that was dedicated in 1908. This church served the Russian community until twelve acres were purchased on North Main Street. In 1974, the cornerstone of the old church was placed at the new.

Across town, the Greek Orthodox church overlooks the highway. Its central dome design represents God's heaven supported by twelve columns representing the twelve disciples of Christ.

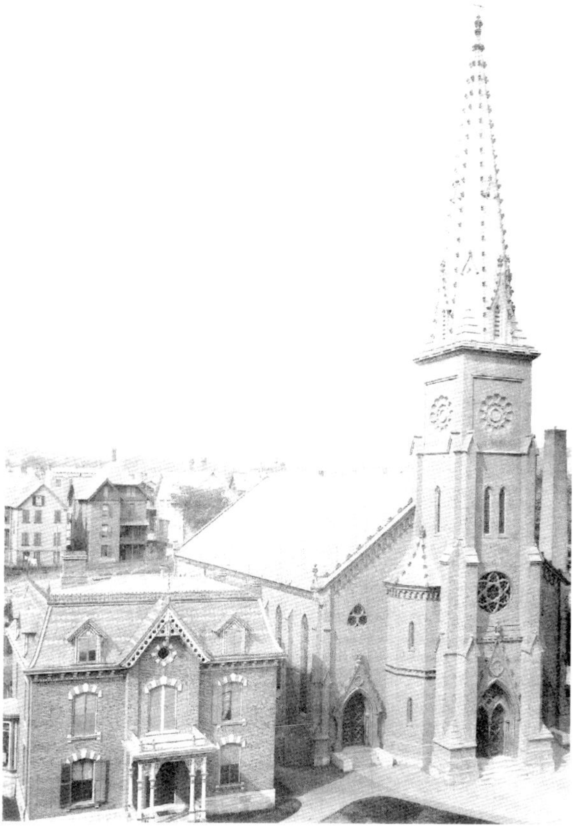

IMMACULATE CONCEPTION Father McGivney's first mass was celebrated on Christmas Day, following his ordination in Baltimore. The Immaculate Conception has since moved and was reconstructed in a different style. *From* Waterbury and Her Industries.

Aside from the Christians, the Jewish population had a large impact on the city's development from the time when the earliest families arrived from Germany. By 1872, forty families formed a congregation of Reform Judaism, with the Eastern European Orthodox Jews following in the 1880s.

The Reform community established the first synagogue at 100 Willow Street in 1921, moving to Williamson Drive in 1957. Recently, that synagogue was discontinued and sold to the Church of Latter Day Saints.

A small Jewish neighborhood sprouted on Canal, Chatfield, Bank and Riverside Streets in Brooklyn. Jews prospered in Waterbury and their numbers grew. In 1900, Beth Israel bought a house in the Overlook section to use as an Orthodox synagogue. Later, a second congregation called Sharis Israel was formed. By 1914, a Hebrew Institute was opened.

A second neighborhood north of the central business district soon filled with Jewish families.

It was during the Second World War that families who had moved up into the Overlook section began planning for a Jewish school. Beth El Synagogue on Cooke Street was dedicated in 1929 but didn't reach completion until 1951, adding its school in 1962. Beth Israel proposed a site near Kingsbury Elementary School on Columbia Boulevard, where construction began much later, in 1961. For ten years the Beth David Academy operated before being sold.

A merger between Beth Israel and Sharis Israel resulted in a new Orthodox synagogue on Roseland Avenue named B'nai Shalom.

The Overlook neighborhood was a pleasant place to raise a family. Jewish children attended religious instruction, and day camp at Fulton Park provided summer recreation. Their family homes were spacious and welcoming.

When the horrors of World War II were exposed, this community actively raised funds for relief and relocation. This population took care of those at home and now would care for those displaced abroad.

In 1938, the year the Jewish Federation began, Waterbury Jews raised $20,000. The Goss home on Murray Street was purchased in 1960 to house the organization, the first to fund nonlocal Jewish causes.

But like other families in the Overlook section of Waterbury, Jewish families began moving to the suburbs. The Community Club that was dedicated in the 1970s was located on the border of Middlebury and eventually sold to Post College for its physical fitness center. One by one the synagogues closed.

But a rich Jewish presence remains.

Handsome homes built for large families and a stately synagogue overlooking a beautiful park beckoned the Orthodox Jewish community of Yeshiva Gedolah in 2000. Nine Orthodox families pioneered the move to Waterbury and garnered a fifty-year lease to use the UConn extension campus that was vacated after the school moved into downtown. The campus sits on seven acres of property formerly owned by the Benedict family, and seven newer buildings for education ranging from kindergarten to college surround its twenty-two-room mansion.

Approximately 120 families have moved into the Hillside and Overlook neighborhoods, filling the school with 90 students in 2001, and grew to a family population of 300 in 2008. The community plans expansion to a fifty-four-lot subdivision off Boyden Street.

One cannot leave the topic of religion in Waterbury without mentioning the attraction of Holy Land.

In 1957, Abrigator Hill (Pine Hill) became the scene of a religious phenomenon that made its mark on the city. Attorney John Greco had a

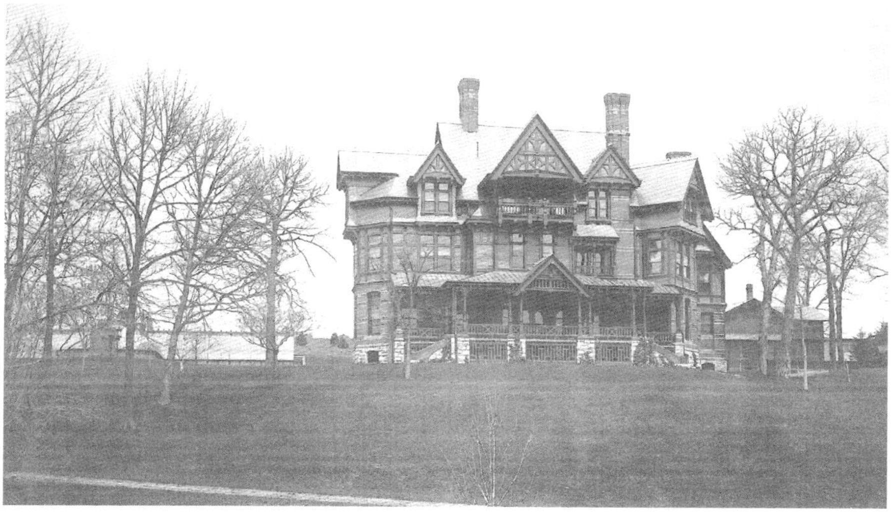

Benedict Mansion
The Benedict-Miller House is a Stick-style Victorian mansion that has been used as part of the UConn extension campus and now serves the Yeshiva Gedolah. *From* Waterbury and Her Industries.

dream, a call from God, to bring the Holy Land to Waterbury. Working with a cadre of volunteers and using donated materials, Greco and his friends constructed miniature dioramas of biblical scenes. Chicken-wire armatures were covered with plaster and grottos appeared, crosses were planted, temples were built and paths were paved throughout seventeen acres.

A thirty-two-foot cross stood at the apex, replaced in 1968 with one having a steel frame that was illuminated and visible from the nearby highway and throughout town.

The roadside attraction was soon attracting more than forty thousand visitors a year, making it necessary to add a parking lot and gift shop.

The park closed in 1984, and Greco soon passed away at age ninety-one, leaving the site to the Religious Teachers Fillipini of Bristol, who have not been able to attend to Holy Land as thoroughly as had Greco. Consequently, vandalism and erosion have taken their tolls, making townsfolk skittish about the future of the site. But when rumors were spread that the nuns were going to dismantle and raze the once-popular tourist attraction, a movement began to "Save Holy Land."

Chapter Eleven

DISCRIMINATION

Waterbury was a town with slaves. Mingo was the first to arrive in 1730, bought by Deacon Thomas Clark. Historian Henry Bronson explained in 1858:

> *His master used to let him out for hire by the day, first to drive plow, then to work with the team. At Clark's death in 1764, Mingo was allowed to choose which of the sons he would live with. He preferred to remain at the old homestead with Thomas; but after the latter commenced keeping tavern, he did not like his occupation and went to reside with Timothy on Town Plot. He had a family and considerable property and died in 1800.*

The low numbers of slaves found in town was a matter of practicality. Long winters meant many nonproductive months for the agrarian community, and feeding an extra mouth was more a hardship than a help.

Mingo was not alone. Other slaves in town were distinguished not only by the color of their skin, but also in possessing only one name. Bronson reveals that Mingo was joined by Dick, Fortune, Dinah, Samson, two named Phillis and Ped.

Dick the Slave was born in Africa, but most of his ninety years on earth were lived in Waterbury as part of Deacon Stephen Bronson's family.

Africans weren't the only ones to grace the slave rolls in Connecticut. Following King Philip's War, local Indians were taken into captivity, and one Native American woman was listed in Waterbury as belonging to the Woodruff family until her death in 1774. Even white men tried and convicted of crimes could be put into bondage.

Waterbury's pro-American position during the Revolution meant supplying soldiers for General Washington. The enlistment of slaves in the Continental army came after British troops promised freedom to any slave joining the English. When Mingo left Waterbury to fight for American freedom, he joined nearly five thousand other black soldiers under Washington's command.

Directly following the Revolutionary War, Connecticut passed an act that limited the time of servitude by slaves, wherein no "Negroes, mulattos, or Indian children" could be held past their twenty-fifth birthdays. This same act outlined punishment for slaves wandering without a pass from their owner or the court and set a curfew of 9:00 p.m.

The importation of slaves to America ended in 1807, when laws were passed to curtail the institution. While this meant that no new slaves would arrive on American soil from elsewhere, slavery outside of Connecticut lived on. Elsewhere in the nation, slavery was for life, and the offspring of slaves were added to the inventory of those living in bondage.

Those years following the Civil War until the migration north of southern blacks are hidden from history, aside from the AME Zion Church, with its 150 members in 1896. When the southern states faced drought, poverty and discrimination, free blacks sought a better life elsewhere. Like other hardworking people before them, southern blacks saw the industrial North as a promised land. Waterbury, with its many factories, was not overlooked in this migration.

The black experience was similar to that of the European immigrants. Men would come and find jobs before sending for their families. Blacks, however, weren't as welcome, and jobs were not easily obtained until immigration limited the number of Europeans entering the country. With that shift, opportunities arose, and by 1920 the city population was 1 percent black. Still, most of the employment was in the unskilled category, and black women were excluded from the factories entirely.

Factories in Waterbury were "open shops." When owners were faced with a dissident workforce and strikes, they turned to black laborers as strikebreakers. Black workers had been denied admittance to trade unions and found that strikes offered opportunity for more employment, a fact that further wedged a rift between white and black laborers.

The seeds of unrest in Waterbury began early in the twentieth century and bloomed during the civil rights movement of the 1960s.

Conditions for the city's black population were substandard. Garbage pickup was not a high priority, and this service was often overlooked in black neighborhoods. Whereas the parks in white neighborhoods were of the finest quality, even the most rudimentary recreational facility was absent for black children. Rents were high and services low, a discriminatory condition that existed for decades.

Improving one's status through hard work was the road to success for immigrant workers, but black laborers were confined to the meanest of jobs and the lowest of pay. Meager savings that would allow for home ownership did not buy a worker and his family out of poverty since the only homes open to blacks were those within the ghettos where they rented.

Still, the conditions in the South were worse and the population of blacks in Waterbury rose. Their neighborhoods centered on Long Hill and Walnut-Orange-Walsh (WOW), with a social life revolving around the Pearl Street Neighborhood House. Bowling, sewing, cooking, sports and dances were the staples at Pearl Street. Churches provided a stable gathering place for families.

Watching white workers achieve much more was a hurt that was hard to bear. A bell had rung for change and Waterbury answered that call. Dr. Martin Luther King had begun a peaceful movement for civil rights in the South, but nobody felt peaceful following his brutal assassination. Blacks across America took to city streets and rioted. Waterbury's North End was one of those cities and the police responded with force.

Time magazine covered the rioting of 1967, reporting:

> *With more than 45 dead in rioting across the nation last week, thousands injured, and upwards of $1 billion in cash and property losses, Americans groped for words to fit the failure. New York's Senator Robert F. Kennedy called it "the greatest domestic crisis since the War Between the States."*

The North End was not rebuilt in a fashion favorable to creating a strong residential neighborhood, and discrimination continued. With jobs decreasing and opportunities for advancement withering, crime and drugs infected the poorest areas.

A change came in 1969, when the federal government used Waterbury as a test case to hone its skills in ending school segregation. This move started in Topeka, Kansas, with the *Brown v. the Board of Education* case of 1954, a case that affirmed that segregation of neighborhoods was de facto discrimination. The government really wanted to target Boston but expected a virulent public outcry.

Waterbury's answer was to create the mega-junior and high school complexes, drawing children away from their neighborhoods to be educated in a desegregated fashion. In hindsight, this move also kept neighborhood schools from being improved in order to reach an equal level and disenfranchised parents from participating in school activities since the distance proved an insurmountable obstacle for those families without cars.

Schools weren't the only battlefields for desegregation. Peter Burns writes, "In the early 1980s, a court ruled that Waterbury's civil service test restricted the number of minorities hired by the city." As a result of this ruling, the city had to hire one minority for every white appointed.

Decades have passed and progress has begun. Black leaders have emerged. From 1991 to 1997, Gary Franks served in Congress for three terms. After serving several terms as alderman, this Waterbury native was the first African American congressman elected from Connecticut.

For Latinos in town, the adherence to Spanish as the language of choice defined that culture. A disagreement heard by the Federal Office of Civil Rights erupted between the city and Latinos in 1996. The city maintained a position that Spanish-speaking students should be mainstreamed, using the bilingual program as a transition to the English language. Latinos argued that the bilingual education should be a part of the education system, where mainstream courses would be offered in two languages. The government agreed that the city's bilingual program did not meet federal standards.

Chapter Twelve

POLITICS

Politics is the word that comes to mind when Waterbury is mentioned. The city has a long and checkered history that has spawned ridicule and angst.

Before the Great Depression, Waterbury's democratic process was not unlike any of the other cities in Connecticut. The city had produced a string of colorful mayors, several congressmen, three governors and one lieutenant governor/mayor. It also produced, from this list, four convicts.

The first to raise a blip on the corruption radar was Waterbury's first governor in 1908, George Lilley. Before taking office, the governor elect was charged by citizen activist George Fox with the misuse of funds, a violation of the four-year-old Corrupt Practices Act of Connecticut. Lilley was later exonerated.

It wasn't until a later administration that the word corruption would become the watchword of the city.

What ended in 1939 began long before T. Frank Hayes took office. The previous mayor, Francis Guilfoile, served from 1922 to 1930, and when he left office, Waterbury's debt was $16 million, with a deficit of $4 million. The Great Depression had begun, and Waterbury was in serious financial straits.

Fiscal reform was Hayes's promise, and the voters bought it, thrusting Hayes into the mayor's office. Guilfoile was ousted, and there were promises of good times ahead. Hayes proved a dashing figure, splendid in his white hats and known for riding a white steed in local parades. He was a ruddy man of quick wit and popular.

The new mayor immediately bonded the $4 million deficit. An audit of the previous administration revealed that Guilfoile had irregularities with contracts, excessive payments to contractors and illegal payments to city officers. The state legislature investigated and found the bookkeeping to be sloppy; though it hinted at criminality, no charges were brought. Hartford welcomed the change in government and was eager to help Hayes reverse the city's financial difficulties.

Hayes assumed office with the hope that he could live up to his promises of reform, and the state granted him leeway to alleviate the burden he inherited. He began by revamping the city charter with a "strong mayor" provision, giving him full responsibility for city transactions, overseeing the ethics of city employees and hiring and firing at will.

With a 41.90 mill rate, the public also hoped that Hayes would prove a good mayor who was able to put the city back on track.

The new mayor proved to be a quick study and implemented changes almost immediately, some of which were hidden from the public's scrutiny. The first of Hayes's victims was education. Approximately 1.5 percent of the mill rate had been set by the legislature in Hartford, earmarked for building schools. Hayes siphoned off that money to the general budget.

When the city had to meet $100,000 for bond payments, Hayes sent the legislature half the amount, banking on its goodwill to fund the rest.

In 1935, Hayes was elected lieutenant governor under Governor Wilbur Cross while still serving as Waterbury's mayor. Two years later, the legislature allowed Waterbury to float $2 million in bonds for the infrastructure. The money was allocated by the WPA and earmarked for work relief, increasing the city's bonded indebtedness to $18 million.

With broad changes that appeared as reform, Hayes's popularity with the voters grew. When he first took office, he garnered a seven-hundred-vote lead that rose to a plurality of nine thousand. By the end of his career as mayor, that lead had dropped seventeen hundred when Sherwood Rowland replaced Hayes's cohort Daniel Leary as comptroller.

This upset was the result of the local paper, the *Republican-American*, investigating stories of employee misuse and the distribution of goods to individuals favorable to Hayes.

Real evidence was made manifest when Sherwood Rowland took office in 1938 with only a thirty-three-vote lead over the incumbent Leary. Rowland armed himself with evidence and met with state attorney Lawrence Lewis to ask for a grand jury and an out-of-town prosecutor to investigate the corruption that was running rampant in city government. Rowland's evidence convinced the state officials and put Hugh Mead Alcorn Jr., Harold Mitchell and country detective Edward Hickey in charge.

Stories began to surface of reprisals against enemies of Hayes and complaints against the city. City employees feared for their jobs. Taxpayers were at the mercy of the city assessors.

The initial findings were enough to empanel an extraordinary grand jury, which submitted a seventy-five-page report and issued twenty-seven arrest warrants.

What was revealed in this report was sickening to the Waterbury voters. The newspaper further revealed that, prior to the election, Comptroller Daniel Leary had promised that he wouldn't expose the findings of a New York detective that might prove embarrassing to publisher William J. Pape and the paper's attorney, Warren Upson. The deal was refused, and stories were printed that led to the subsequent election upset. Later, the paper uncovered voter fraud—registered loyal Democrats were also being listed as Republicans to offset the numbers.

The report issued by the grand jury estimated that the amount of money illegally spent in Waterbury was in the millions. The "rampant corruption" it cited included bribes, payments and kickbacks for imaginary projects and services—self-serving investments.

The trial, which lasted nine months, ended on August 16, 1939, after the jury deliberated for six hours and thirty-two minutes. Actress Rosalind Russell and her brother, James, were spectators in the packed courthouse when the defendants were found guilty.

For decades the Hayes story was linked to the city and had been ingrained in the local lore. It wasn't until the 1990s that Hayes's indiscretions would be topped.

The second half of the twentieth century had a political landscape dominated by the Bergin family. In 1956, Edward D. Bergin defeated the incumbent mayor, Raymond Snyder. This led to a political career in which the Irish funeral home owner vied with Snyder for the top seat in town, earning three to Snyder's two before Bergin died in office in 1969.

Ellyn Bergin Scully remembers the campaigns against Snyder as colorful but gentlemanly. "When my brother Tony contracted polio, my father stopped campaigning during that year's election. Snyder stopped too, saying that if Bergin couldn't campaign, he wouldn't take an advantage."

It was a gentler time, devoid of political dirty tricks and mudslinging, she recalled. With a broad smile, Ellyn remembers, "He was a classy guy. If my father had to lose to anyone it was better it was Snyder."

Bergin's son Edward D. Bergin Jr. (Mike) followed his dad into the mayor's office in 1976.

Waterbury was a bastion of Democrats, and it was not surprising that presidential candidate John F. Kennedy would do a favor for Governor Abe Ribicoff and State Chairman John Bailey and make a quick stop in

Connecticut before returning home to Massachusetts a few days before the election.

It was November 6, 1960, and people began filling the green at 6:00 p.m. to see the young congressman address the crowd at 9:00 p.m. The moment was historic for the multitude of Catholics in town—Kennedy was one of their own. He was a candidate with whom they could identify. Kennedy was of Irish descent, like Mayor Edward D. Bergin. Kennedy hailed from a family of nine children; the Bergin family had nine as well.

The crowd waited and the numbers swelled until the people spread beyond the green. Reporter Sherman London (later editor) from the *Waterbury Republican-American* wrote that despite the cold, rainy weather, the crowd "was the largest mass of humanity" ever to gather downtown. The police estimated that the crowd contained between forty and fifty thousand people.

At 1:00 a.m., Kennedy's plane landed in Stratford amidst a crowd of twenty-five hundred well-wishers. His motorcade wound its way north through the Naugatuck Valley, where people lined the streets to greet him.

It was 3:00 a.m. when the exhausted candidate addressed the Waterbury crowd. "My name is Kennedy and I have come to ask for your support."

Kennedy won in Connecticut by ninety-one thousand votes.

Ronald Reagan hoped to replicate this moment in 1984, when he visited the city for a noon rally on the green. Despite having named Scovill CEO Malcolm Baldridge secretary of commerce in 1980, this president failed to make the same impression.

After this, the city's political future became something distinctive. Mayor Joseph Santopietro toppled the Bergin administration in 1986 after a rift developed in the Democratic Party.

One needs to understand that Waterbury politics is fundamentally about party competition. Peter Burns writes in his book *Electoral Politics is Not Enough* that "party competition is more prevalent in Waterbury…Democrats and Republicans are the deepest of enemies." To prove that Waterbury is a Democratic town, one needs only to look at the numbers: forty-two Democratic mayors to only sixteen Republican ones during the years between 1853 and 2001.

Waterbury's politics had been a conflict between the two largest ethnic groups, with the Irish controlling the overwhelmingly large Democratic Party and the Republicans led by Italians.

The young Republican, a twenty-six-year-old landscaper, appeared to be an unlikely candidate against Mike Bergin, whose father had served as mayor in the years preceding him. Santopietro came armed with the credentials of being a Republican during the Reagan years and fitting the ethnic bill of being a Town Plot resident of Italian descent. He served three terms.

A federal indictment brought against the young mayor cited a meeting with local bankers from the Security Savings and Loan Association, at which a plot was hatched to bilk Waterbury out of money. The charge was that from 1986 until the time he was arrested in September 1991, bankers Richard Barbieri, John Corpaci and Vinal Duncan awarded $170,000 in money, loans and property to Santopietro. Later, news reports cited the amount as high as $700,000.

The corruption involved a complex plot of property loans and leases, and the *New York Times* reported that the indictment said "the developers structured corrupt transactions with the defendant public officials to avoid any promise or appearance of a specific action in exchange for any specific benefit."

According to newspaper reports, the investigation began when the bank fell in the wake of the security and loan upheaval. The wash of corruption spread over several aldermen, a mayor's aide and advisor and the mayor's brother.

Rumors circulated that the mayor had been arrested following an FBI chase through Town Plot.

Santopietro served six years in prison and was forty when he embarked on a new career. In 2006, he reappeared in the news when he, along with his employer James Galante and twenty-seven others, was arrested. The charges stemmed from an FBI investigation into mob ties to the trash-hauling business. Galante owned a trash-hauling company, and the feds charged that money was sent to Matthew Ianniello of the Genovese crime family.

The charges stipulated that money was used for carving out specific territories for trash hauling, thereby cutting out competition from other companies. Santopietro served Galante as a consultant.

Santopietro was sentenced in 2007 to five years' probation and $3,000 in fines but avoided jail in order to care for his children while his wife recuperated from gunshot wounds inflicted during a nasty divorce action in which her client was killed and Julie Porzio Santopietro was shot by the client's ex-husband.

Political rival Edward "Mike" Bergin was reelected following Santopietro's downfall and reassumed the leadership of a city in financial straits. During his seventh term as mayor, Bergin embarked on a bold move—to tear down the old Scovill plant and clean the polluted soil in order to pave the way for a new mall alongside the highway. Some saw his election to office as a rescue mission to put the city back on track, but detractors contended that his administration was rife with cronyism and the continued rise in taxes had driven out the middle class. No rescue would be easily forthcoming.

At this time, the city was still reeling from the exodus of the major brass industries. Unemployment was high. Bergin faced a different scenario.

In 1992, Waterbury's crime rate was double the state average, and 10 percent of the people lived below the poverty level. In 1963, over twenty thousand people were employed. By 1987, that number dropped to the eleven thousand mark. Retail growth diminished by 13 percent.

The American economy had experienced another downturn, and the city's housing market crashed. Some homes in the Overlook area had sold for as high as $179,000 before the market dropped their value to less than half that amount.

The city was on a downward slide similar to other "rust belt" cities. For years, stretching back farther than Mayor Bergin's terms, the social fabric had begun to unravel. A move to the suburbs for workers was followed by "white flight" in the aftermath of the race riots. Cities had a large welfare roll and needed to provide more social services than outlying smaller towns. The city became the repository of social ills, thus making them more unattractive and resulting in a decreasing tax base.

Bergin's tenure followed his 1988 arrest for corruption over towing charges. He was acquitted, but the time and tide of economic woes went against him. In 1995, Philip Giordano replaced him.

Giordano fit the model used to select Joseph Santopietro by the Republican Party in town: he was young, Italian and lived in Town Plot. By profession he was a lawyer who had earned a seat in the state legislature. At the time of his nomination, Republican Cathy Awwad had been campaigning to be mayor. Awwad's experience in local government and as a pharmacist owning her own business had given rise to speculation that she would become the city's first female mayor.

In a surprise upset at the convention, Awwad acceded to the nomination of Giordano.

Giordano won, but his leadership was lacking, and the city began a downward slide that led to a state "takeover."

In 2001, Governor Rowland acted quickly to stave off financial ruin in Waterbury, Connecticut's fifth-largest city. With over $39 million needed to shore up the city's finances, the governor appointed Marc Ryan to run an oversight committee to manage the city's budget. The oversight board comprised a panel representing business, finance, labor, the mayor, the state treasurer's office and a voter. The term was five years (if the budget could be balanced), and its powers were extraordinary.

The board's job was to oversee the finances of city contracts exceeding $50,000; it could set aside existing contracts, would approve the city budget and had authority over labor contracts.

Ryan worked for the governor as budget director at the state capital and was determined to sort out what went wrong with Waterbury spending. The committee's first task was to pare down the city's workforce by 10 percent, but the community was millions of dollars in debt and had a bond standing of scarcely more than a "junk" rating. Labor unions were asked for significant "give-backs" during contract negotiations.

Peter Abare-Brown, director of human resources for the city, noted that "99% of the City of Waterbury workers are union members so having a good relationship with the unions is important. The unions are not going to go away."

He went on to explain that there are laws, called the MERA Act, covering the rights of municipal employees. When faced with an impasse during contract negotiations, management and labor had the right to arbitration by a panel of three. Normally, under this law, the panel would look only at the issues at hand and make a decision based on the last best offers put forth by each side.

The oversight committee's power extended beyond this method and allowed it to bring up issues of its own.

After the real conditions were revealed, the mayor's reaction was a sigh of relief, admitting finally that the job had been too much to handle and blaming the current crisis on thirty years of mismanagement prior to his election.

What the people of Waterbury didn't know was that federal agents were conducting an investigation into local contracts following an investigation in Bridgeport that led to Mayor Joseph Ganim's arrest. A close advisor to Ganim was Paul Pinto, who was also a contributor to Giordano's campaign. Similarities began to emerge. The name of Joseph Pontoriero from Worth Construction in Bethel was linked to both mayors.

Worth had been the construction company to create what came to be known as the Million Dollar Dog Pound. Giordano was seen to be eager to do business with that company and did not tell local aldermen that the company was under suspicion elsewhere. Worth Construction was viewed by New York State and Pennsylvania as a company considered to have ties to crime.

Pinto confessed to kickback schemes in Bridgeport and had ties to Worth. His testimony was instrumental in convicting Ganim.

Seven months after the FBI confronted Pinto, an investigation was opened in Waterbury.

Though nothing out of the ordinary seemed to emerge publicly, there were clues that something was in the wind. When President Bush visited the city, the mayor was conspicuously absent. Word was out that the president did not want to be photographed with Giordano.

Surveillance began on Giordano. Law enforcement bugged city hall telephones and Giordano's car, and a satellite dish was connected to his home to record computer activity. FBI agents spent time listening to what they later called "bizarre" telephone conversations and repetitive calls to women by the mayor. Then a taped conversation caught everyone by surprise.

During the course of the investigation, which federal agents dubbed "Operation Landfill," the mayor had been heard on July 12 planning a sexual liaison with two elementary school–aged girls.

This development derailed the initial investigation as agents reacted swiftly to protect the children from what they believed was a molester. Giordano was apprehended and asked to wear a wire in order to implicate two city contractors in the initial corruption probe.

On July 18, Giordano announced that he would not run for another term as mayor, citing the need for more time with his family as the reason. His wife was not by his side. Giordano spoke with John Murray following the press conference and stated that he "had a weight" lifted from him and that he might pursue a job in Washington. "Now I'm free as a bird," he told the *Observer*'s publisher.

Three days later, the children were placed in protective custody.

The "free bird" was suddenly arrested one morning in New Haven, and the FBI swooped down on Waterbury with warrants waving.

City workers were ordered to leave the building while evidence was taken; workers swarmed through town and into coffee shops to catch their breaths at the development. When word came out about the molestation charges, citizens feared that the city would never recover its pride. And the word did get out—nationally. The media pounced on the crime, and Waterbury quickly became a source of ridicule.

Philip Giordano was convicted in 2003.

For a conservative town with deep family values, this was abhorrent. To make matters worse, a family member had procured the girls. She was reputed to be a prostitute who had conducted a long-term affair with the mayor and fathered a child by him. One of the girls was her child and the other a niece.

Articles were virulent about the crime and subsequent trial, some citing Giordano as "the most reviled person to ever disgrace a public office in Connecticut." Waterbury-born governor John Rowland urged Giordano to resign.

The former mayor, who admitted to accepting payoffs from contractors, received a sentence of thirty-seven years for violating the rights of the youngsters. When Giordano was sentenced, U.S. District Court judge Alan Nevas commented, "This case is the worst I have ever seen…what you did is indescribable."

According to the *Hartford Courant*, prostitute Guitana "GiGi" Jones had employed Giordano as an attorney for a number of years after she was arrested on prostitution charges, paying him off with sexual favors. For her role in providing Giordano with her daughter and niece, she received a ten-year sentence.

Aside from the depravity, the case contained an element of something new. The crux of the prosecution's evidence was the use of a cellphone to arrange for the tryst. The cellphone utilized an interstate device in the transmission of the call.

Alderman Sam Caligiuri assumed leadership of the city until a new mayor could be elected and began addressing the irregularities with the pension fund that had been underfunded and borrowed against.

Into this fray walked Michael Jarjura. He had served the city as a state legislator for a number of years and was known to be a conservative Democrat. His family has a thriving produce business in town.

The oversight board was already in place, creating structural and management changes. "No one had more gratitude and admiration than me," Jarjura recalls. It was stipulated that if the city's budget could be kept balanced for a period of years, the city could resume control of its own affairs. Jarjura proved a stable hand on the city's tiller and fulfilled the requirements on time.

The brink of financial ruin didn't dim the fires of Waterbury politics. Residents were confused and angry over how the city had been run and the knee-jerk reaction was to replace those in power. Despite the city's steady progress with the oversight board, Jarjura faced serious challenges.

The most serious happened in 2005, when he lost a primary election. This was a defining moment for the city, a chance for it to show the world its brass.

Jarjura supporters filled an empty storefront on Wolcott Street, and though the space was large, it was filled with long-term Democrat supporters and newcomers charged with the feeling that this was the defining moment in which citizens could take control. A write-in campaign was launched.

Many of the speakers that night joked that it would be a difficult task, made more difficult because it would mean having to spell Jarjura's name right.

Following the November election, the paper reported:

> *Jarjura won against astounding odds. He had been thumped by Karen Mulchay in the Democratic primary, in September, and was unable to get his name on the November ballot. His only option was to launch a write in campaign. He had to convince the Waterbury electorate that he remained the best choice to lead the city into the future, and then he had to educate the voters how to cast a write-in vote.*

"We got 8,000 voters to write in my name," Jarjura said. "And they did so in a nearly flawless manner." It helped that campaign workers distributed pencils and key chains brandishing the spelling.

Waterbury made the national news with positive coverage. The citizens had made a stand for honest government, and though detractors could cite that Jarjura had not been a steamroller for progress nor a wunderkind of economic development, the city had remained stable and resumed control over its finances.

And Waterbury citizens desperately needed something good.

Prior to Jarjura's victory, Governor John Rowland had resigned his office and was charged with tax fraud. Rowland, whose grandfather had been the whistleblower during the Hayes scandal of the 1930s, had done a great deal of good for Waterbury and other Connecticut cities when he launched a plan for revitalization. During his tenure, the face of downtown changed dramatically. The Rowland Government Center on the green was erected (named for Rowland's grandfather). Along East Main Street, old buildings were replaced with an Arts Magnet School, the UConn Waterbury Branch and the restored Palace Theater.

Rowland's conviction and sentence to a year of prison plunged the city into a new round of despair that was only lifted with the amazing Jarjura campaign.

"It was uncharted territory," Jarjura explains. "We thought it would be a miracle to eke out a win but we got a plurality of 2,000."

Winning, however, is only the first step. Jarjura had to overcome having the highest mill rate for taxes in the state and no promise of economic development coming from outside.

Chapter Thirteen

MODERN TIMES

The city's motto is: *Quid Aere Perennius*. Translated, this means "What is so lasting as brass?" The answer may be grit in the face of adversity.

Endurance through hardship seems to be the true quality of a Waterburian. Early residents persevered through difficulties, making the best of what they had and utilizing the resources to advantage. In the beginning, farms outside of town were thriving. No one knew then that a brighter future was pending. The good times of the Industrial Revolution were only a portion of the city's history.

We are in a similar position today.

The post-write-in period for Michael Jarjura and for Waterbury as a city has been one of impending promise. The recent losses this country suffered economically have put some of that promise on hold, and the question of whether Waterbury will recover is dwarfed by the larger question of whether America can pull itself up by the bootstraps as it did following the Great Depression.

"We are in better shape than other Connecticut cities," Mayor Jarjura maintains. "Times will change and we'll see another wave of prosperity, and if we stay true to the business practices and the government practices, Waterbury will catch that wave."

Citing the overall American economy as experiencing a sea change, Jarjura believes that this is a time for the city to improve neighborhoods and housing, capitalizing on the beautiful assets of Waterbury.

People seem to prefer looking back, looking wistfully at better times that ended with the disappearance of the brass industry. The industry's leaving is explained in many ways—some claim the union demands were too stringent; some blame desegregation. But the decision to move was larger than Waterbury.

No American city could compete with the lower wages offered by third-world countries. Incentives for trade, cheap land on which to build, higher profits and a lack of governmental controls provided corporate leaders with all the reasons they needed. Plus, there was one more push prodding them away.

The American government decided in 1963 that it was time to clean the country. Waterways were becoming nothing more than sewers. The word "smog" entered our vocabulary. The Clean Air Act was passed into law, followed by the establishment of the Clean Water Act. A media campaign began to educate the citizens about the evils of pollution.

Industry feared that it would be held financially liable for removing the pollution it caused. In Waterbury, that would have been a substantial price tag. Environmental concerns were very real in the Naugatuck Valley. According to the website for the Naugatuck Watershed Organization:

> *A report by the state Sewage Commission dated 1899 stated that the Naugatuck River had reached the limit of permissible pollution due to the discharge of industrial wastes and municipal sewage. A subsequent report by the state Board of Health in 1915 described the river as badly polluted throughout its length and listed six municipal and 29 industrial waste sources on the river. This grossly polluted condition was essentially unchanged into the late 1960s and early 1970s.*

In the years prior to the Clean Water Act, the Naugatuck River was essentially dead.

The loss of industry in the Naugatuck Valley, coupled with aggressive measures to control pollution, has helped reverse that trend. Today, the Naugatuck River sports fish and a river walk is planned.

There remains a fear in some, however, that the city will not recover. When Holy Land's illuminated steel cross was recently reconstructed, the smaller, less distinctive replacement seemed to proclaim the city's diminished status. The overriding question becomes, is there hope?

The potential for progress is best seen from above. If we could elevate skyward and look down, a better understanding might be had of Waterbury's place in Connecticut and New England. Waterbury stands as a central point in the state, midway between New York City and Boston, as well as midway between Hartford and New Haven. Its proximity to these larger cities is two hours' highway travel time at the most, a half hour at the least, and it is only a half hour to the shore of Long Island Sound.

The location is wonderfully advantageous, and its roadways remain as important as they were when Washington relied on them during the Revolution. The once dirt-packed roads have been replaced by snaking highways, two of which form a crossroads in town (I-84 and Route 8). The Naugatuck River, the Great and Lesser Brooks and the Mad River still provide waterways through town, and from above, the city sports a smattering of beautiful lakes and ponds.

Coming in closer, one can see that the man-made improvements do not stop with the highway. One of the single most important features of this city is its railroad connection to Bridgeport and on to New York City. Near the train tracks is a glorious array of architecturally important structures that, despite their neglect during the lean times, remain a significant tie to the wealthier past.

The hills that surround the town's floodplain insulate Waterbury in a sense, but this landscape also contributes to a small-town feel, with a green-centered, pedestrian-friendly downtown. It is the largest small town in Connecticut, with a stable population base and a housing market that contains some finely made homes.

The years between the oversight board and this latest economic downturn were spent preparing for the future. The town's city hall is, at present, being restored. The Cass Gilbert jewel piece is a central figure in the ring of other Cass Gilbert buildings surrounding it (the former Lincoln House welfare society, the Chase Dispensary, the Chase headquarters and the Waterbury Bank building). All but two are in private hands and are utilized in functional capacities.

The decision to refurbish city hall was hard-won. It was in dire shape, with the heating system on the wane, the windows rotting and the plumbing on its last legs. It fell far short of meeting the fire codes. A vandal flooded the building. It was up to the people to decide whether it was a building worth saving.

The first time that decision was brought before the people, a referendum was called and the plan was voted down. Subsequent debates over cost and need finally led to a second chance, and the work is in progress. The cost for this over a twenty-year period is $67 million.

Downtown development has been key to the economic plans for improvement since it is the city's most central neighborhood. It is less congested than it has ever been, with many tenements removed during the years of urban redevelopment. In the 1980s, a move was made to create a "Renaissance," and during this period a string of high-end restaurants provided entertainment to the many office workers employed by banks that filled the city center with people throughout the week.

As banks consolidated and moved employees into more suburban settings, office space was plentiful but unused. Without people earning paychecks, retail began to wane.

In 1997, the *New York Times* reported that the former Scovill plant site would be replaced with a shopping mall with direct access to the highway. By the time of its construction, the vacancy rate for downtown had climbed to 48 percent. It was hoped that the more than one million feet of retail space would lure regional shoppers to the area and provide over two thousand jobs to the local economy.

Before the first foundation could be laid, the task of alleviating the pollution began. A total of sixty-three buildings and more than 100,000 tons of contaminated dirt had to be removed, thereby erasing over two hundred years worth of toxicity. The cost of remediation was first estimated at $20 million. With the inclusion of moving the Mad River, that cost rose to $31 million.

When the new mall was introduced, a fear swept through the downtown that it would become obsolete. The fear was realized as many of the long-standing businesses moved to the new mall or closed their doors for good. Insult was added to injury in 1992, when *Money* magazine ranked the city last for its quality of life.

That same year, a downtown landmark was in its death throes. Howland-Hughes had been the last remaining department store continuously operating in Connecticut, owned and operated by three generations of the Paine family. The multistoried market was hemorrhaging customers. Selling the building was near to impossible, and so Hank Paine's answer was to convert the former store into something smaller and focused on Connecticut-made items.

The city was buffeted from many angles, and in one case, tragedy happened far from home. In April 1987, construction workers in Bridgeport were building a sixteen-story residential facility called L'Ambiance Plaza. The plans called for a lift-slab style that, as it turns out, placed too much stress on the floors. When the building collapsed down on itself, twenty-eight men were killed and thirteen were injured. Of the dead, twelve hailed from Waterbury, and of those dozen, ten were members of the community of Italians who hailed from Pontelandolfo, Italy.

Just prior to this man-made disaster, Hurricane Gloria had left its mark in September 1985. Connecticut was the storm's third landfall. With the protection of Long Island, hurricane winds were uncommon in the city. But Gloria had strength and hit the city with eighty-three-mile-per-hour winds. Windows were blown in and branches downed.

As the eye of the storm passed, people braced for a second onslaught that never came. The back part of the storm had died away. In all, seven people died in New England, with one of those deaths occurring in town.

Second to water, wind has been Waterbury's greatest natural enemy. Beginning in 1955, a series of tornadoes often surprised residents as it swept through. That year, an F2 tornado passed near the city, but an F4 barreled over Bunker Hill in 1962. An F3 tornado attacked the downtown, causing one factory to lose its roof and injuring two persons on Main Street.

The most damaging tornado in recent memory occurred in 1989, when a series of three tornadoes ripped through the state, traveling south from Massachusetts to Hamden. The one that passed over Waterbury was measured as an F2 that grazed above the Columbia Boulevard area, toppled the steeple at St. John's downtown and continued south. Power was out for days and telephone service was spotty. For weeks following the storm, workers spent hours cutting away the uprooted trees and downed branches.

The last tornado reported occurred in 1996 and damaged Wilby High School.

Times have been hard in Waterbury. As New York–based businesses began moving into the state, they never traveled up the Naugatuck Valley. Banks began to consolidate, beginning a move out of town as small local establishments evaporated. With the loss of the banks, the attorneys serving them also exited.

The city responded to the economic downturn with development funds to lure Internet-based businesses to town that could utilize upper-story space. The Naugatuck Valley Development Corporation, changed to the Waterbury Development Corporation, launched an Internet Technology Zone that would provide start-up funds, as well as build rehabilitation dollars for technological companies that hired local people.

While some small companies took advantage of the offer, the larger mega-employers weren't interested in the city, and Waterbury would not become another Silicon Valley.

But the drive to instill the downtown with new life continues. UConn relocated to East Main Street, transferring its Hillside Campus to the new Yeshiva community, which wanted to form an Orthodox community in the Overlook section—taking advantage of the historic temple overlooking Fulton Park. The Waterbury Arts Magnet School was erected across the street. The newly restored Palace Theater began operation and provided a lineup of entertainment acts that elicited regional response. The interior is a masterwork of fine craftsmanship. On the night that Tony Bennett appeared as the theater's first act, he demonstrated the quality of the acoustics by singing without a microphone. "Let me show you what a real theater can do," he said. His rich voice carried up and filled the space. The audience was first in awe and then broke into riotous applause, both for the quality of Bennett's voice and with pride.

A move to involve citizens in the restoration of the city began in earnest when the city joined the National Trust's Main Street Program. Dozens of volunteers converged on the Mattatuck Museum to hear the plans for providing economic development. Local merchants banded together to

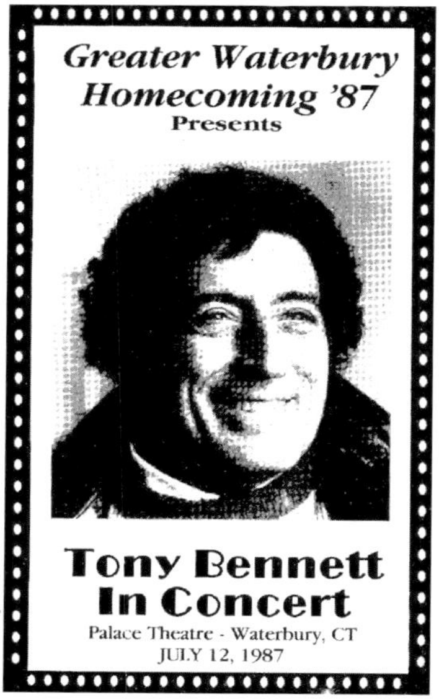

TONY BENNETT
Tony Bennett was the last act before the Palace closed, and he was the first to perform when it reopened. *From the author's collection.*

help in the revitalization. Events were launched to underscore the fact that Waterbury had become a clean, safe, family-friendly urban center.

A walk through downtown today tells a story. One can begin with a visit to the Mattatuck Museum where you can admire the careful blending of old with new architecture. The turn-of-the-century Masonic Hall was transformed in 1984, when notable architect Cesar Pelli incorporated a modern corner façade with geometric pyramid as an entry for the newly acquired museum. The former site sits across the green, a small brick home. Within the museum, one can first visit the new technology-interactive exhibit of the city's history on the first floor before visiting the art gallery above.

Outside the museum is the center green. Gone are the overhanging elms of days past and the bandshell gazebo, but the space remains a lively collective of people and memorials. One of the development moves in years past was to create elderly housing downtown, and residents of these facilities can avail themselves of the green space or participate in the free concerts and farmer's market held once a week.

The churches that make up so much of Waterbury's cultural heritage provide a grandeur and serenity to the streetscape.

Moving south toward the library, the former homes of industrialists are converted to business and city use. State courthouses and a modern library now provide the gateway to the city from the train station. Within the business district is a selection of small shops and empty storefronts. It is hoped that by upgrading the quality of the spaces on upper floors, residential space can be provided to attract new blood. To that end, the WDC assisted the Main Street group with a program of façade development that gave building and storeowners grants to reconstruct their "appearances."

New schools are being constructed in nearby neighborhoods that are currently economically depressed. The WDC has actively engaged in the development of the facilities and the outlying area. In the Brooklyn section, the agency demanded from the state and won the right to retain the historic façade of the old Duggan School. "Keeping the beautiful quality of this school is important," WDC project planner Andrew Martelli remarks. "The state wanted to cut spending but keeping this original design is priceless, it defines the neighborhood."

Moving outward from the city's center one finds a mélange of neighborhoods. Over the years, citizen associations have been encouraged to help improve the quality of life. While condo developments speckle the town, the older neighborhoods retain a "family flavor" to them. Yet some of these have suffered with persistent blight.

Federal money is short in supply, but Waterbury's financial standing in this economic downturn has made it possible to obtain some assistance that will allow us to better prepare for the future. Congressman Christopher Murphy recently garnered $15 million for the city to begin this work, reclaiming the old Chase mill strip along the river in Waterville, which will be reconverted to house the city's street department with enough room to lease space to companies. Another WDC project slated for cleanup and development is the old Mattatuck Manufacturing Company property on East Main Street.

The wave of foreclosures affecting the country did not overlook Waterbury, but federal dollars through HUD will help with the removal of blighted, abandoned houses and restorations that will place families into their own homes.

A bright spot on the city landscape, housed in the old Chase Dispensary, is the Connecticut Community Foundation. It started in 1923 at the behest of local civic and business leaders to help those in need. Today, the organization is a well-run regional foundation that provides grant assistance in a range of areas, offering help to the arts, healthcare, social services, environmental programs and education.

Ironically, our greatest detriment is also our greatest asset. The railroad leading into town is bordered by the brownfields left over from the old industries that utilized rail transport. These brownfields are costly to clean but represent potential for attracting business into the city. The railroad is the key to larger promise. It is hoped that an intermodal transportation center can be constructed alongside the depot, creating parking and a terminus for rail, bus and taxi travel that allows visitors coming into the city to be able to travel anywhere within its confines.

Restructuring the old industrial sites into a mix of business park, recreational areas and residential living can make Waterbury extremely attractive, offering several good colleges to train workers, an available workforce for support positions, a centralized location, affordable housing and property values, an attractive city center and affordable land within an expensive state. With a cleanup of the city, it is possible for Waterbury to compete for jobs in the next wave of prosperity.

There is a national move afoot that seems to agree with this logic. UConn urban studies specialist Ruth Glasser provides a compelling argument for the "third place." According to Glasser and other urban specialists, life is fragmented into three spheres. The first is home and the second is work. The third place is communal, a spot where people gather in a comfortable setting to relax and talk with like-minded individuals. In history, this place has been the club, the local pub or any informal place where you will find people relaxing.

This is a backlash to the movement away from cities and the formation of the nuclear family. While suburbs beckon families to areas with large lawns and small communities, they also insulate people from one another. By contrast, cities offer diversity and diversion. Close living quarters foster friendships and an interdependence with neighbors. Small bars, coffee shops and community groups provide regular access to others in places that are comfortable and secure. What hinders this is the perception of blight and a lack of safety.

A communal, urban way of life is common in Europe, and American culture is getting around to recognizing this need. Gentrification of neighborhoods and reclaiming unused urban spaces are ways to achieve this objective. Some Connecticut cities have capitalized on this desire for residential living, such as New Haven's old Smoothie Garment factory near Wooster Street. This former industrial site has been reconverted to apartments and is fully occupied. Other towns, like Lowell, Massachusetts, have utilized old textile mills for this purpose and met with success.

Waterbury is a bit more challenged because a good portion of its industrial space was subject to pollution, making the cost of conversion higher. But we are not without hope. The most central neighborhood prime for residential living in commercial space is downtown.

With a good plan developed by honest people, Waterbury can map out a path for the future. It won't be an easy road, and the process may take a long time. Despite the public's demand for immediate gratification, Waterbury can take the steps that will create a foundation for building another prosperous future.

BIBLIOGRAPHY

Anderson, Joseph. *History of the Soldiers' Monument*. Waterbury, CT: Waterbury Monument Committee, 1886.

———. *The Town and City of Waterbury, CT*. Price & Lee, 1896.

Bassett, Homer F. *Waterbury and Her Industries*. Gardner, MA: Lithotype Printing and Publishing Co., ca. 1890.

Brass Roots. Waterbury, CT: Scovill Manufacturing Co., 1952.

Brecher, Jeremy, Jerry Lombardi and Jan Stackhouse. *Brass Valley*. Philadelphia: Temple University, 1982.

Bronson, Henry. *The History of Waterbury, CT*. Waterbury, CT: Bronson Bros., 1858.

Bucki, Cecelia. *Metal, Minda and Machines*. Waterbury, CT: Mattatuck Historical Society, 1980.

Burns, Peter F. *Electoral Politics Is Not Enough*. New York: SUNY Press, 2006.

Burpee, Charles W. *The Military History of Waterbury*. New Haven, CT: Price, Lee, & Adkins Co., 1891.

A Century of History in the First Baptist Church. Hartford, CT: Case, Lockwood & Brainard, 1904.

Garrow, David J. *Liberty and Sexuality*. N.p.: University of California Press, 1998.

Glasser, Ruth. "Waterbury, Connecticut: An Evolving Multi-Latino City." Working paper, University of Connecticut.

Guest, Raechel. *Houses of the Hillside Historic District, Waterbury, CT*. Waterbury, CT: Backhus Foundation and Mattatuck Museum, 2007.

Hahn, Mannel. *The Cancellations of Waterbury (Connecticut) 1865–1890*. Chicago: Wm. R. Stewart, 1940.

John W. Hill and the Waterbury Cancellations. Waterbury, CT: Mattatuck Historical Society, 1938.

Liebeskind, Harry. *First Annual Report of the Jewish Federated Appeal*. Waterbury, CT: Rapid Press, 1939.

Monagan, Charles. *Greater Waterbury: A Region Reborn*. Chatsworth, CA: Windsor Publications, 1989.

Pape, William Jamieson. *The History of Waterbury and the Naugatuck Valley*. S.J. Clarke Publishing Co., 1918.

Proctor, Mary, and Bill Matuszeski. *Gritty Cities*. Philadelphia: Temple University Press, 1978.

Rohloff, Paul C. *The Waterbury Cancellations 1865–1890*. Chicago: Collectors Club of Chicago, 1979.

Roth, Matthew W. *Platt Bros. and Co*. Hanover, NH: University Press of New England, 1993.

Silas Bronson Library's Waterbury Hall of Fame Program Book. Waterbury, CT: Waterbury Observer, 1997.

1635–1935 Waterbury Observation Connecticut Tercentenary Program Book. Waterbury, CT: Mattatuck Historical Society, 1935.

Ward, Geoffrey, and Ken Burns. *The War*. New York: Knopf, 2007.

The Western Connecticut Jewish Community Center Dedication Book. White Plains, NY: Monarch Publishing, 1975.

Western Connecticut's Great Flood Disaster. Waterbury, CT: Waterbury Republican-American, 1955.

Internet Sites

anglicanhistory.org
bookrags.com
catholic-saints.suite101.com
chasebrass.com
fathermcgivney.org
fundinguniverse.com
greaterwaterbury.com
highbeam.com
nationmaster.com
nytimes.com
palacetheaterct.org
rep-am.com
scovill.com
time.com
waterburyct.org
waterburyobserver.com
wfsb.com
wikipedia.org

ABOUT THE AUTHORS

Edith Reynolds is a former reporter for the *Waterbury Republican-American* and worked as an assistant editor and writer for the *Litchfield County Times*. She has also written for the *Northwest Hills* magazine, the *Waterbury Woman* and the *New Haven County Woman*. John Murray is the publisher of the local newspaper the *Observer*. They are also the authors of *Wicked Waterbury*.